INDUSTRY AND COMMERCE OF
THE CITY OF ROME

ANCIENT ECONOMIC HISTORY

Advisory Editor
Sir Moses I. Finley

*See last pages of this volume
for a complete list of titles*

INDUSTRY AND COMMERCE OF THE CITY OF ROME
(50 B. C.—200 A. D.)

HELEN JEFFERSON LOANE

ARNO PRESS
A New York Times Company
New York • 1979

Editorial Supervision: Erin Foley

Reprint Edition 1979 by Arno Press Inc.
Reprinted from a copy in the Newark Public Library
ANCIENT ECONOMIC HISTORY
ISBN for complete set: 0-405-12345-0
See last pages of this volume for titles.
Manufactured in the United States of America

Library of Congress Cataloging in Publication Data

Loane, Helen Jefferson, 1907-
    Industry and commerce of the city of Rome.

    (Ancient economic history)
    Reprint of the ed. published by Johns Hopkins
Press, Baltimore, which was issued as ser. 56,
no. 2, of Johns Hopkins University studies in
historical and political science.
    Originally presented as the author's thesis,
Johns Hopkins University, 1938.
    Includes bibliographical references and index.
    1. Rome--Industries. 2. Rome--Commerce.
3. Rome (City)--History--To 476. 4. Rome (City)
--Industries. 5. Rome (City)--Commerce.
I. Title. II. Series. III. Series: Johns
Hopkins University. Studies in historical and
political science ; ser. 56, no. 2.
[DG107.L6 1979]   338'.0937'6   79-4990
ISBN 0-405-12378-7

INDUSTRY AND COMMERCE OF THE CITY OF ROME
(50 B. C.–200 A. D.)

SERIES LVI   NUMBER 2

THE JOHNS HOPKINS UNIVERSITY STUDIES IN
HISTORICAL AND POLITICAL SCIENCE

Under the Direction of the Departments of History,
Political Economy, and Political Science

INDUSTRY AND COMMERCE OF THE CITY OF ROME
(50 B. C.—200 A. D.)

BY

HELEN JEFFERSON LOANE

BALTIMORE
THE JOHNS HOPKINS PRESS
1938

PRINTED IN THE UNITED STATES OF AMERICA
BY J. H. FURST COMPANY, BALTIMORE, MARYLAND

PREFACE

Much that has been written about the economic organization of the Roman world has of necessity been based on the abundant remains at Pompeii, while the scarcity of materials has prevented a detailed study of the trade of the capital itself. Administrative problems arising from the importation and distribution of state grain have been thoroughly treated; the labor guilds at Rome have been studied; references to artisans or tradesmen in the sources have been gathered; and the trade-marks on articles found in the city have been carefully published. In addition, the topography of the ancient city to a large extent has been determined. As yet, however, no attempt has been made to combine epigraphical, literary, and archaeological material into a picture of the commercial and industrial life of this, the largest city of antiquity.

As capital of a vast empire Rome drew its imports from all the known world. On the other hand, since it was the chief residential centre of this empire, it produced relatively little for export, paying for its imports with imperial salaries, the tribute from the provinces, and returns from foreign and Italian investments. A complete enumeration of the imports, their sources, and their carriers would involve all that is known of Roman commerce and the products of most districts in the Mediterranean area; consequently, it has been necessary to select for discussion in the first chapter only the chief articles of trade and the most important sources of supply.

The city was not entirely dependent on imports, for in a society that employed slaves extensively, some articles of consumption—either because of convenience or economy—were always produced in the home. The Romans, furthermore, long continued the old practice of having many of their luxuries or necessities made to order in accordance with individual tastes, and the small shops in which these were manufactured operated at Rome as well as at Pompeii. The suggestion that

industry in the capital was different from that of the smaller
towns has often been based on the change in domestic architecture following Nero's fire, when the atrium style of house
was generally abandoned in favor of the compact and high
apartment-house type. An attempt is made in the second
chapter to define the extent to which this innovation was
accompanied by similar qualitative changes in industrial
quarters.

In an industrial system where the contact between consumer and producer or importer was far more direct than in
modern cities, problems of distribution were relatively few,
and the machinery of distribution relatively simple. A peculiar situation arose at Rome, however, where several of the
emperors intervened in the processes of local trade by building mercantile structures to rent out to retailers, apparently
to increase the facilities for private dealers. In the third
part of the study any additional motives of the state will be
considered.

Roman writers have little to say about the organization of
trade and industry in the metropolis, since the work in shops
and manufactories was generally performed by slaves or
ex-slaves and commerce was still largely in the hands of
foreigners. As a result enterprises of this nature were not the
concern of citizens. No Roman author devoted any single work
to purely economic questions except in the field of agriculture, and all too much dependence must be placed on casual
references in the works of non-specialists like Cicero, Strabo,
Pliny, Tacitus, Suetonius, Martial, Juvenal, Frontinus,
Vitruvius, and Columella.

In the archaeological material there is inherent another
difficulty: Rome has been so frequently rebuilt that most of
the evidence which might have existed has been destroyed.
There is extant the *Forma Urbis Romae,* a ground-plan in
marble made at the order of Commodus following the great
fire; and although the remains are fragmentary and the con-
ventions often defy interpretation, the Plan can serve as a
basis for the discussion of domestic and mercantile architecture. The catalogues of the buildings of the various sub-

regions in the time of Constantine known as the *Curiosum* and *Notitia* are also available, but these are too late to be of particular service. For an interpretation of these ancient materials the topographical dictionary by Platner and Ashby, Lanciani's great plan of the city, Van Deman's discussion of the Sacred Way, Boëthius' articles on domestic architecture, and Lehmann-Hartleben's work on state buildings are invaluable. For recent excavations there are notices in the *Notizie degli scavi* (*N. S.*, hereafter) and the *Bullettino della Commissione archeologica comunale di Roma* (*B. C.*, hereafter).

The chief source material is preserved in the *Corpus Inscriptionum Latinarum* (*C. I. L.*, hereafter). In the various parts of the sixth volume several types are available: the *tituli* placed beneath the burial urns of the ordinary artisans, the records of slaves buried in the columbaria of great households, and the honorary decrees set up to government officials by the working men's guilds. Definite information can be derived from the trade-marks on articles made or found at Rome, published in the fifteenth volume of the *Corpus*. These consist of stamps on bricks produced near the city; inscriptions on lead pipes, lamps, wine and oil amphoras, and jars in which were stored varied food products; and the lead markers attached to shipments of marble and other fiscal products. The inscriptions of the sixth volume were collected before 1916, and those of the fifteenth before 1900, but this material may be supplemented by finds recorded in the archaeological journals after these dates.

Constant use has, of course, been made of the histories of Roman economics by Rostovtzeff and Frank, the work of Waltzing on the guilds, and the discussion by Gummerus on "Industrie und Handel" in Pauly-Wissowa-Kroll, *Real-Encyclopädie* (*P.-W.*, hereafter).

To Professor Frank, who suggested the subject of this dissertation, the author wishes to express her deep appreciation. Acknowledgment must also be made of the generous assistance given by Drs. Evelyn Clift and Vivian Little and by Mr. Roger Edwards in preparing the manuscript.

CONTENTS

9

INDUSTRY AND COMMERCE OF THE CITY OF ROME (50 B. C.—200 A. D.)

CHAPTER I

IMPORTS

Rome, the residential centre of the ruling classes which governed a vast empire, was primarily a city of homes;[1] it manufactured little for export, and for local use only those articles that could not be readily imported or that had to be made to order. Consequently, any attempt to describe the economy of the city must be concerned first of all with imports, and these must include practically all foodstuffs, articles of clothing, building materials, furniture, and household implements—in fact, the bulk of all articles which the Romans needed for sustenance and comfort.

Most of these imports came by sea; for although the roads about Rome were graded and well paved, the immediate neighborhood was generally unproductive and wagons drawn by mules and oxen could not move rapidly enough to bring supplies from any distance. Sailing vessels carried cargoes to Rome from all the hundreds of harbors along the Mediterranean, but they were small,[2] slow in movement,[3] and seldom

---

[1] The population is estimated at about 900,000 in Caesar's day and at well over a million in the second century (Cardinali, " Frumentatio " in Ruggiero's *Dizionario epigrafico di antichità romane*, III, 308-311 [*D. E.*, hereafter]; cf. Kahrstedt in Friedländer's *Sittengeschichte Roms*, IV, 1921, 11-21). Oates ("The Population of Rome," *Classical Philology*, XXIX [1934], 101-106) puts the total at 1,250,000, but his calculations are based on assumptions often unwarranted. Beloch (*Die Bevölkerung der griechisch-römischen Welt*, 1886, 392-412) sets the number at 800,000; Nissen (*Italische Landeskunde*, II[2], 1902, 523-550) estimates between 1,000,000 and 1,500,000.

[2] Miltner ("Seewesen," *P.-W.*, Suppl. V, 922) gives the capacity of the average merchant vessel as 78.8 tons. See also Koster, *Das antike Seewesen*, 1923, 162.

[3] The fastest trip from Alexandria to Puteoli (150 miles from Rome) was made in 9 days (Pliny, *Historia Naturalis*, 19, 3-4), though the ordinary journey usually consumed 20. Pliny (*loc. cit.*) lists the times for other rapid and favorable journeys: from Africa

11

sailed in the winter months when clouds hid the stars that
guided the mariners. As a result, the transportation problem
was always painfully pressing. From the point of view of
imports by sea, moreover, the city lay somewhat too far from
the harbor.[4] Yet the Tiber, Pliny's *rerum in toto orbe
nascentium mercator placidissimus,* not only conveyed to
Rome the products that came in through Ostia but also received abundant food and building supplies from its tributaries, the Anio, the Nar, and the Clanis.[5] For the docking
and storage of these imports ample reception wharves and
storerooms had been provided. Along the river bank from
the Emporium to the Forum Holitorium stretched open-air
markets for special products;[6] eight or more large covered
warehouses were available in the early empire for storage;[7]
and the vast fiscal magazines occupied a large part of the area
of the present Prati di Testaccio.[8]

---

to Ostia, 2 days; from Gades, 7 days; from Hither Spain, 4 days;
from Narbo, 3 days.

[4] In the time of Augustus (Strabo, *Geographica,* 5, 3, 5) ships
either unloaded outside the sand bar beyond Ostia (16 miles down
the river) or discharged cargo until they could be drawn up the Tiber.
The harbor begun by Claudius at Ostia and probably not completed
before 64 A. D. was a primitive affair formed by two curved moles,
a lighthouse between, and surrounded by a few warehouses and
dwellings. This new harbor, two miles from the centre of Ostia, was
connected by canals with the Tiber. Later, Trajan's Portus, an inner
basin of hexagonal shape, offered a more protected place for ships to
rest; it, too, was connected by a canal with the Tiber (see Lehmann-
Hartleben, "Die antiken Hafenanlagen," *Klio,* beiheft XIV [1923],
182 ff. and Wilson, "Studies in the Social and Economic History of
Ostia," *Papers of the British School at Rome,* XIII [1935], 41-68).

[5] Pliny's testimony (3, 54) is strengthened by Strabo's explanation
of why Rome was able to support its population in spite of its location (5, 3, 7). Pliny the younger (*Epistulae,* 5, 6, 12) tells of
products being barged down the river to Rome from his villa near
Tiberinum in the spring. The Tiber was navigable for about 104
miles above the city, but the currents were swift. Gaul, where each
river had its guild of shippers, affords the best picture of river traffic
in the ancient world (see Grenier, "La Gaule romaine," *An Economic
Survey of Ancient Rome,* III, 1937, 481-2).

[6] The Forum Boarium, the Forum Vinarium, etc. The landing
place, the piers, and the steps or inclines leading down to the river
may be seen on fragment 188 of the Marble Plan of 200 A. D. (Kiepert and Hülsen, *Forma Urbis Romae Regionum XIIII,* 1896).

[7] Horrea Lolliana, Seiana, Volusiana, Petroniana, Aniciana, Galbiana or Sulpiciana, and perhaps the Leoniana, Peduceiana, Faeniana,
and Postumiana. See Chap. III, section on Horrea.

[8] Platner-Ashby (*A Topographical Dictionary of Ancient Rome,*

I. FOOD SUPPLIES

Grain. Since the days of the Gracchi, when the state first assumed the responsibility of providing cheap food for the city's poor, the maintenance of an adequate supply of grain was a political and commercial problem of grave importance: each month about 1,200,000 modii of wheat (over 300,000 bushels) were distributed to those on the dole.[9] The government officials in charge of the annona had also to keep on hand a sufficient amount at a fair purchase price for the remainder of the urban population and for the 100,000 citizens of Ostia. To meet such needs Egypt sent to the capital an annual shipment of about 20,000,000 modii [10] and Africa, of 40,000,000 modii:[11] in all, about 15,000,000 bushels each year. If the ordinary merchant vessel of 75-80 tons (10,000-11,000 modii) was used for this transport service, then each summer some 6,000 boats carrying Egyptian and African grain put in at Ostia; and to this number must be added the vessels of merchants from nearby.

At Ostia the members of the barge owners' guild (they

1926, 261) report that prior to 1911 excavations had revealed a two-storied structure 200 m. x 155 m. enclosed by a wall and divided into numerous sections. More recent excavations (*B. C.*, LIII [1925], 279-80 and LIV [1926], 267-8) indicate that the horrea were much larger. Kaufman (" Horrea Romana: Roman Storehouses," *Classical Weekly*, XXIII [1929], 49-54) has collected the ancient evidence and the untrustworthy measurements of medieval travelers. The horrea were built before the end of the republic but because of the restoration made by the Emperor Galba were attributed to him by later authors.

[9] In 58 B. C. Clodius passed a law to give free grain to about 260,000 citizens (Dio, 38, 13; Asconius, *in Pisonem*, p. 15 [Stangl]). By Caesar's day there were 320,000 recipients, but the dictator reduced this number to 150,000 (Suetonius, *Jul.*, 41). The number of 200,000 set by Augustus in 2 B. C. remained fairly constant during the first two centuries. To this total, however, must be added the slaves in the imperial household, the soldiers of the praetorian guard, some veterans, and the members of the guilds of *apparatores*. For a discussion of the problem see Cardinali, 238-41 and Rostovtzeff, "Frumentum," *P.-W.*, VII, 174-177.

[10] Aurelius Victor, *Epitome*, 1, 5-6 (beginning of Augustus' reign). Johnson (*Roman Egypt, An Economic Survey of Ancient Rome*, II, 1936, 481) declares that greater revenues came to Rome after the canals had been put in working order.

[11] Josephus, *Bellum Judaicum*, 2, 383 (probably for the time of Nero).

numbered 258 in the second century) were engaged in bringing this grain the 16 miles up the river.[12]   To the size of
this river traffic in the first century Tacitus (*Annales*, 15,
18) gives valuable testimony in his account of the destruction of 300 barges in the summer of 62 A. D.   At Rome a
vast system of stevedores, grain measurers, and warehouse
guards, under the control of a thoroughly organized government bureau, received and stored the city's food.   The numerous inscriptions of these workers' guilds offer the best
commentary on the size of the import trade.[13]

Although African and Egyptian wheat to a large extent
met the capital's needs, shipments were sent from other
provinces and from parts of Italy.   On the mosaics in the
Piazzale delle Corporazioni at Ostia are mentioned not only
shippers from eight African towns, but also from Gaul and
Sardinia.[14]   To these sources of supply, moreover, Pliny (18,

---

[12] *C. I. L.*, XIV, 251 (see also 250, 252, 4568).   Since these men
were owners of barges (*lenuncularii*), the number of boats in use
may have been two or three times this (see Frank, " The People of
Ostia," *Classical Journal*, XXIX [1934], 487, and Wilson, 63).
There are also records of guilds of *codicarii*, who hauled the freight
to Rome on ox-drawn barges (XIV, 4144: 147 A. D.; XIV, 106: 166
A. D.; in Rome, VI, 1649).

[13] At the harbor town of Ostia were guilds of *saburrarii*, who carried off the sand used as ballast (*C. I. L.*, XIV, 102: 156 A. D.;
448), of *urinatores*, who dived into the harbor to rescue merchandise
that has fallen overboard (XIV, 303), etc.   At Rome there were
guilds of *saccarii*, who unloaded the grain in sacks (VI, 4417: time
of Augustus); of *geruli*, the stevedores (VI, 9438-9; 30882; 36754:
2nd century), of *piscatores* and *urinatores* (VI, 1080; 1872; 29700-
2), of *phalangarii*, who carried amphoras of wine or oil (VI, 7803),
of the *mensores machinarii frumenti publici*, who measured out the
grain to be stored in the warehouses (VI, 85: 198 A. D.; 9626;
33883), of *custodiarii*, who guarded the warehouses (VI, 327: 149
A. D.), and of *horrearii*, the warehouse workers (VI, 682; 30813).

[14] For the inscriptions on the mosaics see p. 662 of the Supplement
to *C. I. L.*, XIV.   The African importers are named on the following:
10, 11, 12, 14, 17, 18, etc.; Sardinian, on 21 and perhaps 19; Narbonese, on 32.   On this last mosaic is a picture of a ship being loaded
from a grain elevator (?).   The function and the size of the portico
is discussed by Calza in *B. C.*, XLIII (1916), 178-206.   See also
Rostovtzeff, *Storia economica e sociale dell'impero romano*, 1933,
186-8.   Although both believe this portico was the official centre of
merchant guilds organized and aided by the state, there is little evidence of governmental control of commerce in the first two centuries
of the empire.   The function of the portico is discussed by Frank,
"Notes on Roman Commerce," *The Journal of Roman Studies*,
XXVII (1937), 74-75.

63 and 66) adds Sicily, Boeotia, Syria, Thrace, and the Cher-
sonese.[15] Along with these foreign vessels there put in at
Ostia ships bearing the fine Campanian wheat, designated by
Cicero as *solatium annonae* (*Leges Agrariae*, 2, 84) and
praised both by Strabo (5, 4, 3) and by Pliny (18, 109).
Campania was also an exporting centre for other grains such
as millet and spelt. From Clusium in Etruria, moreover, a
great amount of spelt was brought to the city on Tiber
barges,[16] and from other sections of Italy came quantities of
rye and fodder for the very considerable number of horses
and animals in the capital.[17]

For the early empire there is no evidence that the state
imposed any control on the independent merchants who carried this grain,[18] though at times inducements were offered
to attract shippers from the more alluring profits to be
gained in the Eastern spice and rug trade. The citizens of
Egypt, owners of the vessels in which state grain was brought
to Rome each spring, had early formed a fleet, which, sailing
from Alexandria as a unit, was convoyed by a detachment of
the Roman navy.[19] Though as late as Nero's day this fleet
sometimes put in first at Puteoli,[20] after the completion of the
Claudian harbor with its extensive system of quays and warehouses, grain ships came directly to Ostia. This building
program of Claudius, dictated by a growing concern for the

---

[15] See Rostovtzeff, "Frumentum," 150-164. According to Scramuzza ("Roman Sicily," *An Economic Survey of Ancient Rome*, III,
349-50), the export of wheat from Sicily was about 2,250,000 bushels
in the early empire.

[16] Columella, *de Re Rustica*, 2, 6, 3; Pliny, 18, 66; Martial, 13, 8.
Grain also came to the city from the Po valley (Pl., 18, 127; Str.,
5, 1, 12: millet; Tac., *Hist.*, 2, 17) and from Umbria (Str., 5, 2, 10:
spelt).

[17] The finest rape came from the district around Nursia and the
valley of the Po (Pl., 18, 130); the best rye, from the Taurini at
the foot of the Alps (*ibid.*, 141).

[18] Columella (1, praef. 20) shows that the state let the grain contracts to free shippers. For private dealers see also Cic., *ad Fam.*,
13, 79; Pliny the younger, *Paneg.*, 29; Suet., *Claud.*, 18.

[19] Johnson, 401. The African fleet was organized on the Alexandrian model in the time of Commodus (Scriptores Historiae Augustae,
Com., 17, 7).

[20] Seneca, *Ep.*, 77, 1. By Pliny's time Ostia was the entrepôt for
vessels from Spain, Gaul, or Africa; Puteoli, for Sicily, Egypt, or the
East (Pl., 19, 3).

safety of Rome's food supply (it was said that on one occasion
there was only enough grain for 15 days on hand: Tac.,
Ann., 12, 43), was but part of that emperor's plans to en-
sure the delivery of the annona. To owners of vessels of
10,000 modii or over (about 75 tons) who worked on call for
the state during a period of 6 years the state offered indemnity
for any losses incurred while carrying out government contracts, and, in addition, special exemptions and privileges
of citizenship.[21] Even to the small Italian merchants who
carried grain from nearby and sold it on the open market
the government, in times of scarcity, had always offered
special bonuses to induce them to sell their grain at Rome
instead of in the smaller Italian towns.[22] References to
such *negotiatores* occur frequently in the historians, and for
one, T. Caesius Primus of Praeneste, there is inscriptional
evidence (*C. I. L.*, XIV, 2852: 139 A. D.) for the source of
his import and its destination.[23]

Wine. Wine, the second most important food item, was
imported in large quantities: a not improbable estimate for
ancient Rome, based on the average annual consumption
of modern Italy, comes to about 4,000,000 amphoras
(27,750,000 gals.).[24] On special days, however, extraordinary
demands were made on the city's wine merchants; Lucullus,
for example, needed 150,000 amphoras (over 1,000,000 gals.)

---

[21] For details see Suet., *Claud.*, 18-19; Gaius, 1, 32; Ulpian, 3, 6.
If citizens, these traders escaped the penalties of the *Lex Papia
Poppaea*; if Latins, they were given the *jus Quiritium*. Freedwomen
were given the *jus IV liberorum*.
[22] Suetonius (*Aug.*, 42) says that in time of scarcity Augustus
regulated the price of grain with no less regard for the dealers and
farmers than for the populace. Tiberius followed this practice (Tac.,
Ann., 2, 87), as did Nero (*Ann.*, 15, 39). See Chap. III, section on
Grain.
[23] Primus was a dealer in Etrurian and Umbrian wheat *notus in
urbe sacra.*
[24] See the article "Italia" in *Enciclopedia Italiana*, 750. The
average annual production of wine in Italy during 1926-31 was 40
million hectoliters. Since Italy imports about as much wine as she
exports, the annual consumption is about 1 hectoliter (105 qts.) a
person per year. In ancient Rome, where wine served in place of
tea and coffee also, the annual consumption would be approximately
100,000,000 qts. Cf. Remark, *Der Weinbau im Römerreiche*, 1927,
82.

for his triumphal banquet,[25] and Caesar at triumphal celebrations—when dictator, after the Spanish victories, and at
his third consulship—distributed amphoras of Falernian and
casks of Chian to all banqueters (Pl., 14, 97). As can be
observed from the brands of wine used for these *congiaria*
from the time of Sulla to that of Augustus, native Italian
varieties were gradually replacing the imports from Greece and
Sicily.[26] A little later Pliny, and then Martial, substantiate
this evidence that Alban and Campanian products had gained
control of the Roman market.

For the most popular of these native wines during the
first century there are three sources of information: the
fourteenth book of Pliny, the thirteenth book of Martial, and
the sherds of wine amphoras found at Rome. Martial's list
is perhaps the most valuable indication of the wines drunk in
the city;[27] for Pliny, who has included numerous foreign
wines, may have used Greek sources, some of them quite out-
of-date. Among the brands named by Martial two of the
first nine are from Campania and seven from Latium.[28]
Pliny's list of the ranking Italian wines (14, 61-64) cor-
responds very closely with this;[29] though the Setine which
Pliny places first ranks fifth with Martial; the Caecuban,
eighth for Martial, is Pliny's second; and the Alban wine
comes second and fourth with Pliny and Martial respec-
tively. Although relatively few of the amphoras in which
the wine was brought to the city have their marks still legible,

---

[25] Pl., 14, 96 (100,000 *cadi*).
[26] See Frank, *Rome and Italy of the Republic, An Economic Survey of Ancient Rome*, I, 1933, 355.
[27] Martial's list (13, 108-125): Falernian must, Alban wine, Sur-
rentine, Falernian, Setine, Fundanian, Trifoline, Caecuban, Signine,
Tarraconian, Nomentan, Spoletine, Paelignian, Caeretan, and Tarentine. In this list (beginning with 106) there are included no Greek
wines but two Gallic wines (from Vienna and Marseilles), and one
each from Sicily, Spain, Crete, and Egypt.
[28] The rich Latian vineyards between Tarracina and Sinuessa were
rivalled by the estates of rich landlords in Campania, where the
popular Falernian, Surrentine, and Calenian wines were produced
(Pl., 14, 61).
[29] Setine, Caecuban, Falernian, Alban, Marsic, wine from Statana
(near Sinuessa), Cales, Velitrae, Privernum, and Signia. Of the 80
varieties mentioned by Pliny in the fourteenth book, two-thirds come
from Italy.

2

there are six that are labelled Falernian,[30] five that carried Aminean (grown near Vesuvius: *C. I. L.*, XV, 4510, 4532-4, 5730), four marked Fundanian (4566-9), and one each marked Caecuban (4545), Alban (4531), Signine (4740), Statanan (4672), and Privernan (4587). Other districts from which large producers sent wine to Rome were, according to the existing jars, Beneventum (4544), Veii (4595), and Bruttium (4590-1).[31]

Workable evidence about the details of the wine trade comes only in the second and third centuries when large wholesalers imported consignments from Spain and Gaul. Most of the amphoras from the Alban hills and the farms below the city near Tusculum must have been brought directly to the homes of the well-to-do or to the stalls of the small market dealers in wagons driven by the owners' trustworthy slave or freedman.[32] There is, however, some indication that large contractors from the city went to the large estates and bought the crop as it hung on the vine. The practice existed in Cato's time,[33] and in Pliny's day the crop of Remmius Palaemon near Nomentum was bought by these wholesalers for 400,000 sesterces ($20,000: Pl., 14, 48-50).[34] The method used by these contractors to distribute the wine to the small dealers is wholly a matter of conjecture. Much of the Campanian wine, however, brought to the wine wharves in "tramp" vessels, was undoubtedly sold directly to the Roman *vinarii* who had come down to the wharves from their shops. Interesting details about this commerce, though

---

[30] *Falernum*: *C. I. L.*, XV, 4511, 4532, 4559; *Falernum Faustianum*: 4553; *Falernum Massicum*: 4554; *Falernum Statanum*: 4672. See Remark, *De Amphorarum Inscriptionibus Latinis Quaestiones Selectae*, diss. Bonn, 1912.

[31] To this archaeological evidence must be added two other popular Italian wines known from the sources: Marsic wine (Pl., 17, 171), and the brands carried down the Adriatic from the Picene fields (Str., 5, 4, 2).

[32] There is evidence from the second inscriptions at times found on these jars that they were at times carted back to the farms and used again.

[33] Cato, *de Re Rustica*, 144. See Day, "Agriculture in the Life of Pompeii," *Yale Classical Studies*, III (1932), 192.

[34] See, however, Mickwitz ("Economic Rationalism in Graeco-Roman Agriculture," *The English Historical Review*, LII [1937], 585-7), who discusses this expensive experiment in model farming.

on an extraordinary scale, are suggested by Petronius' account (*Satyricon,* 76) of Trimalchio's mercantile adventures. For the first enterprise Trimalchio himself built five ships, loaded them with wine (*et tunc erat contra aurum*), hired captains for them, and sent them off to Rome. The boats and the cargo, valued by Trimalchio at $1,500,000, were lost in a storm. Undaunted by this disaster, he prepared a second shipment which, in addition to wine, included bacon and beans from his estates near Capua, slaves, and a quantity of the famous Campanian perfumes. From this deal $10,000,000 were realized, if one wishes to believe Trimalchio.

A further development in the marketing of these Campanian wines is indicated by the inscription *C. I. L.,* XV, 4597: Ve(suvium?) C . . . M. l. et soc(iorum). Here a partnership, perhaps of owners of adjacent small estates, has been formed to provide for shipment of the wine to Rome.[35] Certainly, it is an established fact that two-thirds of the villas in the district about Vesuvius had extensive provisions for producing large quantities of wine and oil: 23,000 gallons of wine and 1,300 of oil could be stored in the dolia in the cellar at Boscoreale.[36] There is the further consideration that about 22 per cent of these large villa-owners were imperial freedmen; they would naturally direct their large trading enterprises to the city.[37]

---

[35] It is unfortunate that most of the names on the amphoras found at Rome cannot be identified with either merchants or growers known from other sources. There are, moreover, certain difficulties inherent in the inscriptions (*C. I. L.,* XV, 4529 to 4685), for a name in the genitive may be either the grower or the consumer, and often there is a name of the slave who produced the commodity. An amphora has been found, however, near the Praetorian Camp (4592) marked *Surr(entinum) Clod(ianum) novum,* Surrentine wine imported from the estate of a Clodius, possibly in the vicinity of Stabiae. There were two wine growers at Pompeii with the name of Clodius: Clodius Clemens and P. Clodius Speratus (Day, 207, nos. 39 and 40). Perhaps also Cn. Junius Arabus (a jar of whose aged Aminean wine came to Rome [4534]) was one of the Junii well known as ediles and villa owners at Pompeii (*ibid.,* 208, no. 53). It is even possible that L. Volusius Saturninus, the consul of 3 A.D., had an estate in Campania where wine and garum were produced and apples grown (4559, 4646, and 4784).

[36] Carrington, *Pompeii,* 1936, 89. Also see Table A in Day, 200 and 183-6.

[37] Day, 178-9. The imperial family apparently owned the potteries where the amphoras and *dolia* were made.

For this first century there is little evidence for the importation of wines from abroad, although by the time of Augustus Baetica had begun to ship the cheaper brands to Rome.[38] Two jars in the city labelled Baeter(r)(ense) (XV, 4542-3) also testify to some Gallic import at this time, although the current of trade in this commodity ran rather from Italy northward.[39] Cisalpine Gaul exported wine from near Verona (Str., 4, 6, 8) and the brand stored in urban jars marked *Maritimum* (4662-3). Raisin wine came from Crete (Mart., 13, 106), acid wine from Africa (Pl., 14, 16),[40] and a few fine brands from the East—Berytus, Tyre, and Clazomenae (14, 73-4). Furthermore, the fragments of a jar from the early empire marked *Autocratum* (4539) support Pliny's testimony (14, 78) that the importation of Greek wines continued.

By the middle of the second century, however, Spanish wine (and also oil) had captured the Roman market: some indication of the volume of this commerce is given by the mound of many million clay jars behind the ancient docks, known as Monte Testaccio.[41] Fortunately the jars, none of which have remained unbroken, are inscribed with unusually detailed information about the progress of the wine from the private estates in Baetica to the warehouses at Rome. Taking a typical inscription (XV, 3954), we find that the jar when empty weighed 94.5 Roman pounds, and when filled 215.5

---

[38] Str., 3, 2, 6. This traffic is proved by the presence of two amphoras in the city marked Laur(onense) (*C.I.L.*, XV, 4578-9).

[39] For the apéritifs from Baeterrae (a colony of Narbonese Gaul), Marseilles, and Narbo see Pliny, 14, 68. The wine from Vienna and Marseilles was on sale at Rome (see n. 27). In the second century, particularly the second half, French merchants shipped wine to Italy (Grenier, 533-9, 580).

[40] Tiberius preferred the grapes from the smoky African smithies to those of Verona and Raetia (*ibid.*).

[41] The mound is in the form of a truncated cone about 140 ft. high and 3500 ft. in circumference at the base. If, as seems likely, the fragments of a single broken cask occupy on the average about 1 cu ft., there are over 40 million amphoras in the heap. Dressel (*C.I.L.*, XV²) has published about 800 inscriptions found on the jars and 3,000 stamps on the handles. The Spanish origin of the jars has been discussed by Frank, "Notes on Roman Commerce," 72-79, and "On the Export Tax of Spanish Harbors," *American Journal of Philology*, LVII (1936), 87-90.

pounds; this is about 2.5 times larger than the normal amphora.[42] There is no record in this case of the pottery kiln where the cask was made, but the potter's trade-marks on other jars (see the published handles, XV, 2558 ff.) indicate that many of them were made in Baetica very near the vineyards;[43] some may have been produced on the estates themselves. This same inscription also declares that the cask, worth 24 sesterces (about $1.20), was received at the customs office at Carteia. The receiving clerk here has recorded not only the number of the consignment, the value, and the weight (which he has checked) but also the date, the company of shippers, L. Marius Phoebus and Viator and Restitutus Vibii, and the estate of Attius Cornelius from which the cask was sent. Phoebus and the Vibii, who now own the wine, convey it through Ostia to the Emporium by the Aventine; here the contents of the huge cask are emptied into the smaller amphoras brought hither by the retail *vinarii,* and the ninety pound jar, whose return journey to Spain would be costly, is broken and discarded.

Since there is considerable variation in the inscriptions, several of the items need further comment. The value of the wine, in this case 24 sesterces, ranges on other jars from 20 to 40 sesterces, somewhat lower than the price of 15 sesterces the amphora (of eighty Roman pounds) which Columella (3, 3, 8) quotes as the wholesale price for ordinary Italian wine. The export tax, however, is another factor which must not be disregarded in comparing prices; for although it does not appear on the inscription under discussion, it can be found on about 90 of the other jars. This tax, ranging from 2 to 4 asses (72 are marked áá and only 1 ááá), is approximately 2.5 per cent of the value of the contents, the normal tax on Spanish goods.[44] This tax, of course, precludes the assumption that the wine came from imperial estates or as tribute in kind from public lands;

---

[42] See Festus (p. 312, Lindsay). These jars of Spanish wine ranged from 180 to 220 Roman pounds.
[43] So Hübner, *Ephemeris Epigraphica,* IX (1905), 158-60.
[44] See Frank, "On the Export Tax," 87 f. Also *C.I.L.,* XIV, 4708.

furthermore, when after 217 A. D. wine is exported to the
account of the fiscus, the tax disappears.[45] Mention must
also be made of the location of the chief forwarding stations,
for Carteia—even if the restoration on the inscription discussed is correct—appears very infrequently: Hispalis is
named on 96 jars, Corduba on 49, Astigi on 35, and Gades,
Malaga, and Portus (Portus Gaditanus) on a smaller number. The wine fleet usually sailed from the ports of Gades
and Malaga.

Among the shippers who operated between these ports
and Rome was S. Fadius Secundus, a distinguished citizen
of Narbo whose name appears on 25 sherds.[46] Although
Secundus filled all the official posts in his native city and
was able from the profits of his business enterprises to be-
queath 16,000 sesterces to the carpenters' guild at Narbo
(C. I. L., XII, 4393: 149 A. D.), his discarded cognomen of
Musa would seem to indicate freedman stock. It has also
been pointed out that at least half the ship-owners whose
names are recorded on the jars were of like origin and the
suggestion made that the full freeman's status had been
gained as a reward for transporting foodstuffs to the city
in accordance with Claudius' decree.[47]

In addition to these Gallic shippers the names of four
Spaniards engaged in this trade are known with certainty,[48]
and in view of rather numerous inscriptions referring to
Spanish merchants at Rome (C. I. L., VI, 1625b, 1935,
9677, 29722) it is not unlikely that they carried the bulk
of this import. Another interesting group mentioned on the
fragments are the companies of shippers composed of four or
five men, often patrons with their freedmen, who in all prob-

---

[45] C. I. L., XV, 4097-4141. See Frank, "Notes," 74, n. 5. Sep-
timius Severus confiscated extensive estates in Spain.

[46] The identification was first pointed out by Héron de Villefosse
("Deux armateurs Narbonnais," Mém. Soc. Antiq. de France, 1914,
153 ff.). On XV, 3867, 3868, 3870 and 3873 the port of Astigi is
recorded or implied. P. Olitius Apollonius is the other Narbonese
named on the sherds.

[47] Frank, "Notes," 77-79. See also n. 21 of this chapter.

[48] C. I. L., XV, 3762-9: D. Caecilius Hospitalis (cf. C. I. L., II,
1474) and D. Caecilius Maternus; 3897: M. Julius Hermes (II,
1481); 3852: C. Ennius Ennianus (II, 1195).

ability owned and operated a small fleet of wine ships between Spanish ports and Rome.[49] Women too, who had probably inherited ships from fathers or husbands, were encouraged by the profits in Spanish wine to continue their work (XV, 3691, 3729, 3845-7, etc.)

The numerous sherds of wine jars has made it possible to trace the gradual shifting of the city's supply of wine: after the middle of the second century Campanian and Alban brands carried in farm wagons or on small " tramps " were replaced by cheaper Spanish wines brought on larger vessels by wealthy wholesale merchants. Later in this century and especially during the next, organized guilds of wine importers appear on the inscriptions; there are groups operating on the Adriatic (*C. I. L.*, VI, 9682 and 1101)[50] as well as on the Tyrrhenian Sea (XIV, 131)[51] and guilds specifically designated as bringing wine for the Ostian and Roman markets (XIV, 409, 430, 318).[52] Entire guilds of importers from regions along the Adriatic demand some explanation. Among the wines from these regions that of Pucinum near the Timavus had been brought into favor by the Empress Livia, who declared that she never drank any other (Pl., 14, 60); perhaps the taste for this wine, stimulated by a desire to endorse the fashion of the imperial house, had grown to such an extent that the demand at Rome was very great. Other brands from the " Upper Sea," how-

---

[49] 3730: quinque sociorum; 3788-90: the Caecilii and their liberti; 3844: the Cornelii and their liberti (?); 3984-5: the socii quattuor Pompeii.

[50] L. Scribonius Januarius (VI, 9682) is designated as *negotians vinarius item navicularius, curator corporis maris Hadriatici*: wholesale wine dealer and ship-owner, supervisor of the guild operating in the Adriatic (see Dessau's note on XIV, 409 for Ostian origin). Another inscription from Ostia (XIV, 409) indicates that wines from Picenum, Raetia, and the Po valley were being imported by the middle of the second century, even before the activities of the *negotiantes vini Supernatis et Arimin(ensis)* (VI, 1101: 251 A. D.).

[51] *Negotiantes vini Infernatis*. These importers would carry wines from Campania.

[52] Waltzing (*Étude historique sur les corporations chez les Romains*, 1895-1900, II, 97) declares that there were two guilds of wholesale wine dealers—*ab urbe* (XIV, 409) and *fori vinarii* (XIV, 430): the one supplying the markets of Rome, the other those of Ostia. As proof he notes that Cn. Sentius Felix was president of the *corpora vinariorum urbanorum et Ostiensium*.

ever, were highly praised.[53]   At Aquileia, where the Pucine wine was certainly brought, there were large groups of dealers engaged in trading with the north as well as with the south;[54] so it is not unlikely that these guilds from the Adriatic carried on a flourishing exchange trade at Ostia with wines from Spain or Campania.   To judge from the important positions held by their patrons, the groups were both wealthy and important, but no information can be gained from the inscriptions about their activities.   Within a short period, by the middle of the third century, they had become instruments of a government which had gradually assumed the function of the sale of wines.

Oil.   Because of the many and varied uses of oil an estimate of the annual import is difficult to make.   In his discussion of the economy of Sicily, however, Scramuzza has suggested some figures which may prove useful for comparison: according to his account a slave needed about 1.75 gallons of oil each year for food and a freeman, about 2 gallons.[55]   In terms of the population of Rome this means an annual import of about 280,000 amphoras (1,700,000 gallons) for food alone.   In addition, many thousands of gallons were used for lighting, for the gymnasia, and for the baths.[56]   Furthermore, on extraordinary occasions such as triumphal celebrations thousands of amphoras had to be available within the space of a few days for free distribution.   At his triumph Caesar used 50,000 amphoras (Suet., *Jul.*, 38), though it is possible that this oil was part of the tribute in kind which he had laid on Lepcis.[57]

The Romans of Martial's and Pliny's day still considered

---

[53] Pl., 14, 67; Str., 4, 6, 8.   Vergil (*Georg.*, 2, 95) compares the Raetian wines favorably with the Falernian, and Augustus (Suet., *Aug.*, 77) preferred Raetian wine to all others.

[54] Remark, *Der Weinbau im Römerreiche*, 82 and 97.   See also Str., 5, 1, 8.

[55] "Roman Sicily," 271-2 (based on Cato, *de Re Rust.*, 58).   He also estimates that a Sicilian household used 3 gals. yearly for illumination.   See Pease, "Oleum," *P.-W.*, XVII[2], 2460-9.

[56] In the gymnasium at Tauromenium from 195-167 B. C. 1,004 gals. were needed each year (*I. G.*, XIV, 422).

[57] Caesar (*Bellum Africanum*, 97) speaks of a tribute of 3 million lbs. yearly.   Cf. Plutarch, *Caesar*, 55.   For other distributions see Suet., *Nero*, 12; Tac., *Ann.*, 14, 47.

that the finest oil was produced at Venafrum on a branch of the Volturnus (Mart., 13, 101; Pl., 15, 8; cf. for an earlier period Str., 5, 3, 10); this oil, renowned for its aroma, had the trade-name *Licinianum* and reached an unusually wide market.[58] The trade-name implies production on a considerable scale; indeed, wholesale dealers like the hypothetical Licinius can be found as early as the time of the elder Cato, who tells of contractors buying the fruit from the trees, harvesting it, putting the olives through the press, and disposing of the product (*de Re Rust.*, 144). These amphoras from Venafrum, floated on barges down the Volturnus, probably came into Ostia on Campanian vessels carrying other produce. Considerable quantities of oil, however, must have come from more southern districts in Campania, especially from the estates around Pompeii.[59] In Latium the two most important oil centres were Anagnia and Casinum, both situated on the Via Latina: at Anagnia was a guild of *capulatores* (pressers or skimmers)—an index of considerable production, since one such skilled workman was sufficient for an ordinary farm (*C.I.L.*, X, 5917); for Casinum, there is striking literary testimony.[60]

Even at this period, however, African and Spanish oil was well known in Rome, and in the next century these two provinces supplied most of the needs of the imperial city.[61]

---

[58] Pease ("Ölbaum," *P.-W.*, XVII², 2009) gives evidence for this popularity.

[59] "Ölbaum," 2003. Day (170-2) says that in about 32 *villae rusticae* were provisions for making wine, olive oil, or both. In the cellar of the famous villa at Boscoreale were 12 dolia used for storage; this implies an annual production of about 4,000 gals.

[60] Macrobius (*Saturnalia*, 3, 16, 12, quoting Varro): optima fert ager Campanus frumentum, Falernus vinum, Cassinas oleum, etc. Vergil (*Georg.*, 1, 273) gives a memorable picture of the farmer driving his donkey laden with oil and fruits to town.

[61] Juvenal (5, 86-91) speaks of the sharpness and odor of African oil, and this testimony is supported by finds of handles of oil amphoras in the city (*C.I.L.*, XV, 2633, 3382-5 from Lepcis; 3375-81 from Hadrumetum; 2634 and 2635-6 from Tupusuptu). For Spain, Martial insists that Corduba is more prolific than Venafrum (12, 63; 12, 98. Cf. Pl., 15, 8). West (*Imperial Roman Spain: the Objects of Trade*, 1929, 16) declares that during the first three centuries the amount of olive oil exported from Spain exceeded that of any other province. See also "Ölbaum," 2003, for references to Spanish oil at Rome.

By Hadrian's time there were so many urban dealers selling
African oil and grain that they had organized themselves
into a large and rather important guild (VI, 1620); a
similar group of merchants specializing in Baetic oil is
known from the time of Marcus Aurelius (VI, 1625b).[62]
It may be that these *negotiatores olearii* received and distributed the cargoes brought by Spanish and African shippers to the docks near Monte Testaccio.[63]

The numerous varieties of table olives that reached the
city are in no way indicated by the few extant jars marked
alba dulcis (*C.I.L.*, XV, 4802), *salitas* (?) (4804), and
columbares (stored in their own liquor, 4803); even for
these, however, no source is given, though the most probable
is Venafrum. Martial mentions the import of olives from
Spain (7, 28) and Pliny from Syria (15, 15), but the olive
most sought by the rich and poor alike came from the
Picene Fields.[64] Ships coasting down the Adriatic, carrying
wool from Padua or wine from Aquileia, brought this food
through the Straits and up the coast to the city wharves.
Pliny adds that olives from beyond the sea (Syria, Spain,
and Egypt), although inferior to Italian grown for making
oil, were preferred for the table (*ibid.*).

Vegetables and Fruits. In addition to oil, wine, and the
monthly five modii of wheat, the diet of the ordinary citizen
required some fresh fruits and vegetables, which came to
a large extent from the small truck farms just outside the
city or from the market gardens covering the nearby Alban
and Sabine hillsides.[65] There is also the testimony of the
younger Pliny (*Ep.*, 5, 6, 12) for considerable traffic down
the Tiber from more distant farms along its banks: *omnes*

---

[62] In VI, 1935 is named a *mercator olei Hispani ex provincia
Baetica.*

[63] One of the most prosperous of these shippers was C. Sentius
Regulianus (VI, 29722), a Roman knight and a native of Lugdunum,
who engaged not only in the Gallic wine trade but was *curator* of a
guild importing Baetic oil.

[64] Pl., 15, 16; Mart., 1, 43, 8; 4, 46, 12; 4, 88, 7; 5, 78, 20; 9, 54,
1; 11, 52, 11; 13, 36, etc.

[65] Cicero leased the garden of his estate at Tusculum to a market
gardener (*ad Fam.*, 16, 18, 2). For the splendid orchards about
Tibur see Horace, *Carm.*, 1, 7, 13-14; Propert., 4, 7, 81; Col., 10, 138.

fruges devehit in urbem.[66] Besides these regular supplies
special leeks and cabbages from Aricia [67] or the apples and
pomegranates from Nomentum (Mart., 13, 42) were brought
in wagons down the well-paved roads to the municipal retail
markets.[68] Another open-air market by the river, the Forum
Holitorium, received shipments carried by Campanian vessels—cabbages, beets, radishes, asparagus, and onions.[69] Amphoras marked *mala Campana* (XV, 4783-4) which made
their way to the shop of one of the Roman fruit dealers
(*pomarii*: VI, 9821-3, also 37819) bear indubitable testimony to this traffic. Furthermore, apples and pears from
Picenum (Hor., *Serm.*, 2, 3, 272; Str., 5, 4, 2) were shipped
to the capital.

The exotic fruits mentioned so frequently by Martial and
Juvenal may either represent foreign plants acclimated to
Italy and growing nearby [70] or preserved fruits from Syria or
Asia conveyed to the city in huge conical jars.[71] The *pruna
et cottana* of Juvenal (3, 83; cf. Mart., 7, 53; 13, 28 and 29)
were certainly imported from Damascus; [72] but the Chian
figs that Martial purchased in the Subura (7, 31) and the

---

[66] Pliny's villa was situated near Tiberinum in Umbria. See Col.,
1, 2 and the elder Pliny, 3, 54 for further evidence of traffic on the
upper Tiber.

[67] Pliny (19, 110) names Aricia, Ostia, and Egypt as the places
where the best leeks were raised.

[68] See Chap. III, section on Markets. Aricia was situated on the
Via Appia some 15 miles from the city and Nomentum on a branch
of the Via Salaria about 13-14 miles to the north.

[69] See Day, 175. Pompeian cabbages and onions were famous (Pl.,
19, 140; Col., 12, 10). Martial indicates other vegetables that
reached the city: turnips from Amiternum (13, 20; cf. Col., 2, 10),
asparagus from Ravenna (13, 21; cf. Pl., 19, 151), beans from Egypt
(13, 57), and leeks from Tarentum (13, 18).

[70] The introduction of foreign fruit trees in the period from Sulla
to Augustus is discussed by Frank, *Econ. Surv.*, I, 366. Carian figs
were acclimated at Alba in the reign of Tiberius (Pl., 15, 83).

[71] Olck, " Feige," *P.-W.*, VI, 2100. The figs from Damascus were
the best in the world (Pl., 13, 51; Col., 5, 10, 11); other fine dried
figs came from Lydia (Pl., 15, 69) and Africa (*id.*, 15, 82), but
there were about twenty-nine varieties cultivated in Italy, especially
near Pompeii and Herculaneum (Fronto, *ad M. Caes.*, 2, 5; Pl., 15,
70). In the villa at Domicella was a trench used for drying fruits
(*N. S.*, 1929, 199-203).

[72] In 70 A. D. peaches imported from Asia were rare and expensive
at Rome (Pl., 15, 39-40: a denarius each).

Syrian pears (5, 78) probably came from a farm " within the third milestone."

Cheese. One of the most remarkable cargoes brought down the coast to the Vegetable Market were the 1,000 pound cheeses from Luna (Pl., 11, 241; Mart., 13, 30). Equally prized were the ewes' milk cheeses shaped like pyramids that were carried on Tiber barges from Sassina in Umbria.[73] The origin of the goats' milk for the cheese smoked in the Velabrum (Mart., 11, 52; 13, 32) is not known but it was probably the Sabine farms; Pliny adds that the cheese was " made " at Rome (11, 241). Vestinum on the Via Valeria was an important source of supply (*ibid.,* and Mart., 13, 31), and it is not unlikely that some of the cheese factories in the villas about Pompeii exported to the city.[74] Imported cheese also came by sea from Gaul, Bithynia, and Liguria.[75]

Meats. For members of the poorer classes a bit of salted meat was all that was required for the ordinary diet; the fresh meat added on festal occasions was a special delicacy. Much of this salted pork was imported from transmarine provinces: in Strabo's day the ships that carried Belgic *saga* to Rome also brought Gallic pork (Str., 4, 4, 3) ; the Sequani of the valley of the Saône in particular exported large quantities.[76] Swine fed on the acorns from the great oak forests in the Po valley supplemented the capital's meat supply (*id.,* 5, 1, 12), and bacon from the left bank of the Rhine gained a name at Rome (Mart., 13, 54). Moreover, from the end of the republic live swine from Lusitania (Varro, *de Re Rust.,* 2, 4, 10) as well as hams and bacon from the north of Spain were shipped to Rome.[77] Pigs, however, could be raised any-

---

[73] Mart., 1, 43, 7; cf. Pl., 11, 241. Cow's milk was rarely used for cheese (Kroll, "Kase," *P.-W.,* X, 1493).

[74] Carrington, 96. A large cheese factory has been found in the agricultural establishment in the Sarno valley.

[75] Pliny (11, 240) says that the cheese from the mountainous regions north of Nîmes was especially prized at Rome, so also that from Bithynia (242).

[76] Pork was the favorite meat at Rome (Orth, " Schwein," *P.-W.,* III, Zweite Reihe, 809).

[77] Swine were raised in the oak forests of the Ceretani in the extreme northeast of Spain (Mart., 13, 54; Str., 3, 4, 11). For imports from Turdetania in the south see Strabo, 3, 2, 6.

where, and the market gardeners just outside the city walls as well as the farmers in the surrounding plains and the Alban hills found at Rome a ready market.[78]

Sheep, lambs, and kids from neighboring fields were driven down the Appian Way to the district of the Porta Trigemina or barged to the cattle exchange by the river. Although beef and veal were of less importance for food, Domitian's edict of 70 A. D., *ne boves immolarentur* (Suet., *Domit.*, 9), was undoubtedly prompted by concern for the city's food supply. Strabo suggests that in the Augustan period there was a considerable export from the Sabine territory (5, 3, 1), and references to the steers and flocks of Mevania in Umbria are numerous.[79] Perhaps the chief Italian centres for exporting meats may be inferred from those districts which in a later century supplied them for government doles: Bruttium, Lucania, Campania, and Samnium.[80] From across the Straits, too, Sicily continued to send its cattle and hides to Rome and other parts of Italy.[81]

In the earlier empire the farmer who drove his cattle to town probably acted as the distributing merchant, for it was only when the state had established the meat dole (after 200 A. D.), that the trade was organized and large guilds of importers appeared. One importer of beef (*mercator bov-[arius]*), however, a free citizen, is known from the late republic (*C. I. L.*, VI, 37806), and the guild of *mercatores pequarii* who dedicated an altar to the goddess Fortuna of Praeneste (XIV, 2878) may have been concerned with urban trade. More important than these brief records is the inscription of M. Antonius M. f. Claudia Teres, a citizen of Misenum, who is known as a *negotiator celeberrimus suariae et pecuariae* (VI, 33887). Teres' work as a middleman for the farmers near the city had brought him such wealth and in-

---

[78] A pork delicacy from Ostia enjoyed a vogue (Apicius, *de Arte Coquinaria*, 7, 4, 1), and Lucanian sausages were well known (Mart., 4, 46, 8; 13, 35; Apic., 2, 4).

[79] Vergil, *Georg.*, 2, 146; Lucan, 1, 473; Statius, *Silvae*, 1, 4, 128.

[80] The evidence is collected by Waltzing, II, 89-96. See also Scherling, "Italia," *P.-W.*, Suppl. III, 1267.

[81] Scramuzza, 280. Rome and Italy could absorb all the "cattle, hides, wool, and the like" (Str., 6, 2, 7).

fluence that he had been honored with every municipal office in his home town.[82]

Honey and Condiments. Rome's sugar import came in the form of honey, which was used not only for preserving fruits and sweetening wines but in the making of cakes and marmalades of all kinds. A list of Apicius' recipes for cakes made with honey alone would suggest the amount consumed annually.[83] Verres, during the three years of his office, sent 400 amphoras (about 2,800 gallons) to Italy, though these shipments offer no reliable basis for calculating the Sicilian export to Rome.[84] Mt. Hyblas, from which most of Verres' honey probably came, produced a grade highly esteemed in the capital,[85] even if the honey of Hymettus and Pentelicus ranked first during the early empire.[86] These three brands surpassed anything that Italy had to offer, being superior to the honey of Tarentum.[87] By chance the name of one dealer in honey at Rome has survived, A. Fuficius A. l. Zethus (*mellarius a Porta Trigemina, C. I. L.,* VI, 9618), who had his shop near the docks where imported wares arrived.[88]

---

[82] It is noteworthy that Teres imported the meats most popular in the city—pork and mutton. After 200 A. D. special open-air markets were established at Rome for the slaughter and sale of these animals, the Forum Suarium and the Campus Pecuarius (Chap. III, section on Meats).

[83] See Schuster, " Mel," *P.-W.,* XV[1], 372-3.

[84] Cic., *in Verr.,* 2, 183 and 2, 176. Scramuzza (282) discusses the passages.

[85] Mart., 13, 105; 9, 26, 4; Varro, 3, 2, 12; Pl., 11, 32.

[86] Pl., *loc. cit.;* Mart., 13, 104; 7, 88, 8.

[87] Macr., *Sat.,* 3, 16, 12, quoting Varro: optima fert ager Campanus frumentum . . . mel Tarentum, etc. For the cheap brands from Sardinia and Corsica see Mart., 9, 26, 4; 11, 42, 2.

[88] A whole guild of dealers in roses and violets (*violaries, rosaries, coronaries*: VI, 30707 and 169) attests the importance of the trade in flowers brought each day to the city from the nearby suburban estates and the villas around Tibur and Tusculum. In the garden on Cicero's estate at Tusculum, which was leased out to a skilful *holitor* for cultivation, was a spot for growing choice flowers (*ad Fam.,* 16, 18, 2) ; and Varro, it will be remembered, listed the profits from raising roses for sale in the city (1, 16, 3). Probably some exotic flowering plants came by sea from Campania (Campanian flowers best for garlands: Pl., 21, 29) or from the territory around Paestum, the richest spot in Italy for the growing of roses (Mart., 12, 31, 3; 9, 60, 1). The author of the *Periplus (The Periplus of the Erythraean Sea,* ed. Schoff, 1912, sec. 49) even mentions chaplets of sweet clover transshipped from Alexandria to Rome, and Martial

Numerous amphoras filled with the fish sauces in demand
at the capital (*garum, liquamen, muria,* and *halex*) came on
Spanish vessels bringing wine and oil. Trade in these condiments was highly profitable since the best brands, for instance
the *garum sociorum* prepared from the scomber in the fisheries
of New Carthage, were very costly.[89]   According to the inscription found on sherds at Rome, the *socii,* a firm which
bought the fishing concession from the state, packed and distributed its own products; that it did not enjoy a monopoly
in the making of *garum* is proved by the names of independent
shippers which appear on jars carrying this article from Malaga (XV, 4737-40) and Gades (4570).[90] At Rome, moreover,
there was a guild of *negotiantes Malacitani* (VI, 9677), which
maintained a sales depot for fish sauce from Malaga packed
by this group: the *socii,* then, directed their cargoes to repre-
sentatives of the guild who managed all details of distribution.
These dealers had elected as their president a Greek freedman, P. Clodius Athenio, himself a dealer in *salsamenta*:
sauces, dried fish, and condiments of all kinds.

The products of the famous *garum* factory of Umbricius
Scaurus near Pompeii would certainly be brought to the
Roman market,[91] although the fragments of only one amphora testify to Pompeian imports (*garum Pompeianum,* XV,
4686). It is possible, however, that the A. A. Atinis, sherds
of whose jars of *garum* and *muria* have been found in great
numbers at Rome, were citizens of Pompeii.[92]   *Garum* from

---

speaks of the roses, probably in pots, that arrived from the Nile in
winter (Mart., 6, 80).

[89] Pliny (31, 94) gives the price of half an amphora as 1,000 sesterces ($50). A large jar has been found near the Praetorian Camp
marked *halex sociorum* (*C. I. L.,* XV, 4730). Next to oil *garum*
was the chief export of Baetica (Zahn, "Garum," *P. W.,* VII, 841).

[90] There is also the possibility that the merchant (C. C. H.) who
exported *garum flos Lucretianum* (XV, 4691, note) was the wine
dealer C. Consius Hermeros, whose name appears on Testaccio sherds
dating from 149-161 A. D. (3828). The Licinii, whose *garum* was
stored in jars 4689-90, may have some connection with the importers
of wine or oil, S. Licinius Ripanus and M. Licinius Maternus (Testaccio sherds, 3930-1 and 3929).

[91] Frank (*An Economic History of Rome,* 1927, 259) distinguishes
the branches of the factory.

[92] Dressel in his discussion of *C. I. L.,* XV, 3639-40 states that the
name A. Atinius Crescens appears on an unedited Pompeian amphora.

Puteoli (XV, 4687-8) and *liquamen Antiatinum* (XV, 4712) also arrived at the city markets. Many cheaper brands of fish sauces and dried salt fish were imported for the everyday food of the lower classes.[93] The Spanish salt fish ranked first (Str., 3, 2, 6) but was almost equalled by the *tarichos* from the Pontic coast (*id.,* 7, 6, 2).

Fish and Fowl. Of the other food delicacies imported in any quantities, birds and fowl, oysters, and fish were the most important. Dealers in ducks and fattened hens are recorded in the inscriptions (VI, 9200, 9201, 9674), and there is abundant comment in Varro and Pliny about the aviaries and game preserves on rich suburban estates. Seius of Ostia made 15,000 denarii ($3,000) a year on his peacocks alone (Varro, *de Re Rust.,* 3, 6, 3), and his record was equalled by M. Aufidius Lurcio.[94] For those who could afford them the famous oysters of the Lucrine Lake (Mart., 13, 82; 6, 11, 5; Str., 5, 4, 6) were hurriedly brought to the city by the overland route, while those from the promontory of Circeii were shipped the short distance up the coast (Pl., 32, 6). Distant varieties from Spain, Illyricum, Cyzicus, and even the British Isles (*ibid.*), also came by sea route, possibly in large tanks. Although the poor were satisfied by the fish of the Tiber,[95] the rich demanded the rare turbots and mullets which they bred in their private pools [96] or bought from com-

---

[93] See Orth, "Kochkunst," *P.-W.*, XI, 951 and Besnier, "Salsamenta," Daremberg-Saglio, *Dictionnaire des antiquités grecques et romaines* (*D.-S.*, hereafter), 1022 f.

[94] Varro (3, 6, 1) says he made 60,000 sesterces (cf. Juv., 1, 143, with Mayor's note). For other birds eaten in the city see Martial's *Xenia* (13, 58-77): heathcocks from Ionia, doves, wood pigeons, partridges, geese, guinea fowl, etc.

[95] Cf. the *piscatrix de horreis Galbae* (VI, 9801), who probably sold river fish, and the *piscator* recorded in VI, 9799. Other dealers are mentioned in an inscription from Ostia (XIV, 409: *piscatores et propolae*) and in a Roman inscription from the third century A.D. (VI, 1872: *piscatores et urinatores*). See Stöckle, "Fischereigewerbe," *P.-W.*, Suppl. IV, 461.

[96] Pliny (9, 170) says that the fish in Lucullus' preserve at Naples were sold for $200,000 at his death, and Cicero, it will be remembered, often spoke of the rich senators as the *piscinarii* since they were more concerned with their rare foods, represented by their fish, than with the state. Sicilian lampreys were brought alive to Rome to be fattened in such pools (Varro, 2, 6, 2).

mercial *vivaria* in the immediate vicinity of Rome.[97] Strabo, moreover, speaks of two other important sources of supply: the fisheries at Cumae (5, 4, 11) and those off the coast of Etrurian Populonia (5, 2, 6); in addition, along the coast from Ostia to Campania the admiral of the navy under Claudius had planted the scar to furnish food for the city (Pl., 9, 62). Specialties that came from other sources are enumerated by Martial: gudgeon from the Venetii (13, 88), lamprey from the Straits of Messana (13, 80; Pl., 9, 169; Juv., 5, 99-100),[98] bass from Istria (13, 89), and prawn from Minturnae (13, 83).

II. CLOTHING

Three principal centres supplied the city with the woolen cloth from which ordinary togas and tunics were made: the valley of the Po, especially the region around Padua; the territory of the Sequani in Gaul; and the southern Italian districts of Apulia and Calabria. Not only did the extensive mills of Padua send to Rome great quantities of cloth but even rugs and manufactured articles of all sorts.[99] Martial describes some of the triple-twilled tunics from here that could only "be cut with a saw" (14, 143),[100] and Strabo gives a few details about the expensive carpets and deep-

---

[97] See *N. S.*, 1924, 55-60. A large *vivarium* where rare fish were raised for commercial purposes has been discovered near the vigna di S. Carlo dei PP. Barnabiti just outside of Rome.

[98] According to Juvenal, Sicilian fishermen were regularly employed in supplying the Roman market with lamprey and mullet. In 4, 15 he speaks of a 6-lb. mullet costing as much as 6,000 sesterces ($300; cf. Suet., *Tib.*, 34), but the normal price was about 1 sesterce a pound.

[99] Str., 5, 1, 7: "And the quantities of manufactured goods which Padua sends to Rome to market—clothing of all sorts and many other things—show what a goodly store of men it has and how skilled they are in the arts." Other centres in the Po valley were Milan (famous for its linen as well as woolen goods: *C. I. L.*, V, 5923, 5925-29, etc.), Pollentia (noted for its dark wool for the making of slaves' clothing: Mart., 14, 157 and 158; Pl., 8, 191), Brescia (workers in wool: *C. I. L.*, V, 4324, 4501, 4504-5), Verona (linen weavers: V, 3217; woolen cloaks: Mart., 14, 148), Mutina (renowned for its soft wool: Str., 5, 1, 12), Altinum (Mart., 14, 155; Col., 7, 2, 3), and Parma (Mart., 2, 43, 4; 14, 155).

[100] Martial (*ibid.*) declares that the best wool came from Apulia (cf. Pl., 8, 190), the second grade from Parma, and the third from Altinum. Cf. Kroll, "Lana," *P.-W.*, XII, 610-614.

3

napped blankets (5, 1, 12). Cheaper blankets, however, and rough blouses for workmen and slaves in the city were imported to a large extent from Gallic districts;[101] mattresses, too, from this country had so completely captured the Roman market that in Pliny's time the various types were distinguished by their Gallic names.[102]   In the third place, from Canusium, one of the Apulian centres, came the brown wool in which Martial declared most of the city's slaves were clad.[103]   With the more prosperous citizens, however, the white woolen togas from Tarentum in the neighboring district of Calabria and cloaks from the famous Tarentine golden fleece enjoyed great popularity.[104]

Although the inhabitants of the capital, at least during the first three centuries, used very little linen for clothing,[105] flax was commonly employed for bath towels, napkins,[106] wagon covers, awnings,[107] sails,[108] and nets.   Some of these products came from Italy, especially from Cumae and the region of the lower Tiber (Pliny, 19, 10); others from Spain, especially Saetabis and Tarraco.[109]   The cities along the coast of Syria were also engaged in shipping linen cloth of special character to Rome.[110]   Since the days of Rabir-

---

[101] Str., 4, 4, 3; Mart., 1, 53, 5; 4, 19; Juv., 9, 27-9; Pl., 8, 191. Mart., 6, 11, 7: Me pinguis Gallia vestit.

[102] Pl., 8, 192.   Wool imported from the Leucones was used for stuffing pillows and mattresses (Mart., 14, 159; 11, 21, 8; 11, 56, 9).

[103] Mart., 9, 22, 9; 14, 127 and 129; Pl., 8, 190; Varro, Lingua Latina, 9, 38; Str., 6, 3, 9; Suet., Nero, 30.   Apulia was to a large extent given over to large sheep ranches.

[104] Other places which supplied heavy cloth for Rome are mentioned in the sources, though with less frequency.   In the time of Augustus, numerous ships from the land of the Turdetani (near modern Seville) came to Ostia laden with the famous Spanish black wool (Str., 3, 2, 6).   A century later Martial also speaks of a Baeticarum pondus acre lanarum (12, 65, 5), and of mantles in the city made from the cheap Spanish cloth.   (In nine epigrams he mentions the wool raised near Corduba and Gades.)

[105] Olck, " Flachs," P.-W., VI, 2477 ff.

[106] Cf. Catullus' napkin from Saetabis (12, 14; 25, 7).

[107] For the amphitheatre in Caesar's and Nero's day (Pl., 19, 23-24); for private houses and for shops (Juv., 8, 168).

[108] Sails were made in Gaul among the Cadurci (Pl., 19, 8).

[109] According to Pliny (19, 9) the best linen in Europe came from Saetabis.   For Tarraco see id., 19, 10, and for workers in flax at Emporia, Str., 3, 4, 9.

[110] Materials brought to the sales depot of the Tyrians (statio) are discussed in n. 203.

ius' venture with Egyptian wares, however, expensive exports
from the temple estates and the mills around Alexandria
formed part of the cargo of numerous Egyptian vessels putting in at Puteoli and Ostia.[111]

Other vessels from the East brought luxury fabrics that
even the most skilled slaves of the wealthy households could
not reproduce. There were silks woven at Berytus and Cos
(Pl., 9, 25; 11, 76-7), fine fabrics from Laodiceia (Pl., 29,
33), damask from Alexandria (8, 196), muslin from India
(*Periplus,* 63), and embroidered coverlets from Memphis
(Mart., 14, 150). It is probable that Bassus' $500 cloak
(Mart., 8, 10) came directly from Tyre, and it is implied that
Cato's $40,000 table covers (Pliny, 8, 196) were made in
Phrygia. The tapestries woven with gold threads from the
looms of Anatolia, moreover, enjoyed wide popularity.[112]

Because of the changing meaning of the term *negotiator*
it is often difficult to distinguish the importers of cloth from
the larger retail dealer.[113] The imperial freedman, Ti. Julius Secundus (*C. I. L.,* VI, 9670), who is designated as a
negotiator lintiarius (dealer in linens), probably did not make
the trip to Alexandria himself but contracted with an Egyptian *navicularius* to furnish him with a consignment once or
twice during the year. At its arrival he may have sold the
cloth to owners of small shops, who flocked to the wharves,
and thus fulfilled, to a certain extent at least, the functions of
a commission merchant. It is possible, on the other hand,
that Secundus himself bought his stock from one of the warehouses by the docks or from the cargo of a newly arrived
Eastern vessel.[114] The position of M. Aurelius Flaccus *negotians siricarius* (dealer in silks: VI, 9678) can be determined with no greater certainty. Since, however, C. Pettius
Celer (VI, 9431), a dealer in clothing made from Eastern

---

[111] Cicero (*pro Rab. Post.*, 40) speaks of the arrival at Puteoli of
the commercial fleet of the king of Egypt with a cargo of paper,
linen, glass, and " showy " articles.

[112] This vogue was at its height in the Augustan period (Pl., 8,
196; 33, 63; 37, 12; Propertius, 2, 32, 12; etc.).

[113] Cagnat, " Negotiator," *D.-S.* See also Chap. III, n. 35.

[114] The other urban *lintearii* (VI, 7468 and 9526) were probably
weavers; these inscriptions are late.

furs,[115] was of Babylonian origin (the signs of the zodiac on his tombstone are indicative of this), it is possible that he arranged with one of his relatives in the old country to send to him directly a shipment of pelts on a vessel carrying other products. Records of wholesale dealers in woolen clothing, however, are somewhat more definite. The Celtic cognomina of the four *sagarii* (dealers in woolen blouses and cloaks) who were freedmen of L. Salvius suggest that they were importers rather than retailers.[116] Then there are the two freedmen, L. Arlenus L. l. Demetrius from Cilicia and L. Arlenus L. l. Artemidorus from Paphlagonia (the nationality is proudly stated on the inscription, VI, 9675), who probably formed a partnership engaged in the import and retail business: Demetrius was the *negotiator* and Artemidorus the *mercator*.

To shipments of clothing from abroad or from the chief centres of large-scale production in Italy must be added the homespun brought to Rome from the surrounding countryside. In this there was considerable traffic, for Columella assumes that it was a general practice for farmers to raise sheep and for slave women to spin and weave (12, 3, 6). Moreover, if we can accept the amount of cloth prepared on Atticus' estate in Epirus as indicative of activities of large households in sheep-raising districts, these spinning women were not often idle.[117] It is not necessary to suppose, however, that all the steps concerned with finishing the cloth ("fulling") were done at home. There is evidence that homespun from the villas around Pompeii was sent to the fullers of the city, and it is probable that considerable amounts came to Rome to be finished.[118] According to the account of Suetonius (*Aug.,*

---

[115] At Ostia there were entire guilds of *pelliones* (furriers), probably importers (XIV, 10, and 277).

[116] *C. I. L.*, VI, 7971, 37378, and 37774. The four cognomina— Theuda, Ascla, Gatta, and Nasta—are listed in Holder, *Alt-celtischer Sprachschatz*, 1896-1922. The name Theuda (Teuda) is found at Padua (V, 3058), that of Ascla (Ascula) at Verona (V, 3257), and Gatta at Rimini (XI, 483). Cf. n. 99.

[117] The woolen cloth woven on his ranch of 800 sheep (Varro, 2, 2) not only supplied Atticus and his slaves but was even sent to Cicero (*ad Att.*, 11, 2, 4).

[118] The system at Pompeii, in which the fuller served as the entrepreneur, probably resembled the early English method (Frank, *An Economic History*, 262).

73) Augustus tried to revive the practice of wearing clothing entirely prepared at home by setting himself up as a model, but the attempt was unsuccessful; in Columella's time even the farmers' wives scorned the making of their clothing (12, praef. 9).

From the inscriptions, however, only two merchants engaged in bringing such cloth—finished or unfinished—to the city are known. One is Q. Alfidius Q. l. Hylas, a *negotians lanarius* from Forum Semproni (*C. I. L.*, XI, 862); Hylas, who was also a member of a guild that supplied sand for amphitheatres and the building projects at Rome, had apparently reaped no small profits from his two cargoes. There is also the record of L. Nerusius Mithres (XI, 4796), a dealer in goat skins from the Sabine territory, *notus in urbe sacra*. Mithres, like Hylas, had accumulated considerable wealth from his trading with the capital city. He explains his material success in lines 5 and 9 of his epitaph: "I offered goods that suited the popular taste; and in all my dealings I was fair and without duplicity."

III. BUILDING MATERIALS

Stone. Although Strabo noted the large quantities of building material readily available for the city (5, 3, 10-11), he neglected to say that much of it was of a very poor quality. Outcrops of volcanic tufa existed all along the Anio, and blocks of travertine from below Tibur could easily be barged down this branch of the Tiber.[119] According to the same geographer, moreover, the stone from the quarries at Gabii was of great service to the city (5, 3, 10), for because of its fire resisting qualities it was remarkably well adapted to the construction of the fronts of houses.[120] The massive wall of the Forum of Augustus, the outer walls of the Tabularium, and many of the sewers had also been built of this

---

[119] These quarries were used extensively from 100 B. C. to 64 A. D. After the disaster of this year, however, travertine became less popular because it was incapable of withstanding fire. The "red stone" was in use from 140 B. C. to 150 A. D.

[120] Tacitus (*Ann.*, 15, 43) says it was used in great quantities after 64 A. D.

material in Strabo's day. In addition, lava for paving stone was found just three miles outside the city, and abundant quantities of sand for plaster or concrete could be obtained from near at hand.

The size of the traffic in these building stones during the early empire may be illustrated by two sample cases. Over 100,000 cu. m. (about 200,000 tons) of travertine were transported for the exterior of the Colosseum within the period of three or four years. On this basis Cozzo has calculated that 150-180 wagons were probably used each day to carry this material.[121] The transport of a comparable amount of tufa (3 miles out), of brick, and of concrete (the lime would come down the river from the Sabine hills) must also be considered.

An estimate of the materials (mostly tufa) needed for the Claudian aqueduct, based on the measurements of Ashby,[122] shows that approximately 450 cu. m. were used to construct one tier (9.65 m. from centre to centre). As the structure sloped quite consistently over a distance of 10 km. from 25 m. to ground level, the total of about 300,000 cu. m. (600,000 tons) is a reasonable approximation. We know, moreover, that this structure was built within a period of 14 years at a total cost of $17,500,000 (Pl., 36, 122).

Bricks. Satisfactory materials for the making of bricks also existed close by. The well-known reddish pink bricks of volcanic ash from the time of Hadrian were apparently made from the deposits of alluvial clay along the Anio. The fine clay of the Vatican near the Horti Domitiae, however, which had probably served at an earlier period, could not have been used extensively after the days of Nero when the industry finally reached its height. Furthermore, the names of certain yards in the vicinity of the city enable us to locate groups of kilns on the Viae Salaria, Nomentana, Aurelia, and Triumphalis. It is impossible to estimate the size of the quantity

---

[121] Cozzo, *Ingegneria Romana*, 1928, 212 and 98. For the drays in the city see Juv., 3, 254-5, and Mart., 5, 22, 8. The deep ruts in the lava paving blocks in the Via Sacra bear witness to the heavy traffic.

[122] Ashby, *Aqueducts of Ancient Rome*, facing 240.

of bricks sent to the city from these factories; but since during the period 123-155 A. D. there were 46 separate kilns, with as many foremen, in the possession of the wife of Annius Verus alone, an enormous output is indicated.[123]

Marble. Marble for the imperial building program was carried to Ostia on special ships from private and state quarries throughout Italy and the provinces. In his tirade against the importation of luxurious building materials Pliny speaks generally of the extraordinary vessels built to carry marble (36, 2), but gives details only in the case of the ship which Claudius sank at Ostia to form the foundation for part of his new harbor: this vessel, which had brought a monolith of red granite from Egypt in Gaius' reign, had carried 30,000 bushels of lentils as ballast and was 150 Roman feet long (about 1335 tons; Pl., 16, 201-2). A ship such as this was, of course, unusual.[124] Smaller boats, on the other hand, came in great numbers from Carystus in Euboea bringing blocks of the very popular white and green-streaked cipollino; in fact, there is a record of a 2400th shipment of this marble, possibly on a single contract.[125] The rich golden-yellow giallo antico from Chemtou was imported on boats that sailed from Thabraca in Numidia.[126] Other ships carrying marble from Synnada in Phrygia brought the translucent pavonazetto with its rich purple markings.[127] From Iasos in Caria

---

[123] See Chap. II for a discussion of brick production.

[124] Miltner, "Seewesen," 292. Van Buren, "Obeliskos," *P.-W.,* Sonderabdruck, 1937, 2.

[125] For a discussion of the source, use, and quarrying of marbles see Fiehn, "Steinbruch," *P.-W.,* VI, Zweite Reihe, 2278 ff. and Dubois, *Étude sur l'administration et l'exploitation des carrières dans le monde romain,* 1908. Bruzza (*Annali dell'instituto di correspondenza archeologica,* XLII [1870], 118 ff.), who published the sigilla on the blocks of marble in existence at Rome in his time, declares (140) that cipollino was found in greater quantities than any of the other 43 varieties; so Dubois (115-16), who gives the number of shipments. The marble was especially used for colonnades, veneer for walls, and floor covering. The 149 known sigilla date from 17 to 135 A. D.

[126] The markers on these blocks date mainly from the reigns of Hadrian and Antoninus (Dubois, 33-4).

[127] The markers are from 68 to 164 A. D., though the quarries had probably passed to the imperial estates at the death of Agrippa (Dubois, 81).

came the red porta santa,[128] and from Luna to the north of Pisa, the white and mottled, bluish-gray Carrara marbles.[129] Egyptian boats brought quantities of granites, basalts, and porphyries to Rome's harbor town.[130]

At Ostia members of a special guild of *trajecti marmorum* (*C. I. L.*, XIV, 425) transferred the blocks to Tiber barges to be carried to one of the two marble wharves at Rome. The earlier Marmorata was situated by the Tiber in the district of the Aventine; the great wharf on the Campus Martius above the Aelian bridge had been built in the time of Augustus to serve the needs of his vigorous building program in that section of the city.[131] Here the blocks, after being removed from the barges on rollers, were lifted by large cranes from the side landings to the top of the causeway. Near the wharves in the Aventine district were the government offices where the markers which had been attached to the blocks at the mines by slaves of the imperial procurators were checked by special *tabularii*. Private stone-cutters who bought their material from the government found it convenient to locate their workshops close by, for sales of state-owned marble to private artists or builders were made at these offices.[132]

---

[128] The markers date from 67 to 179 A. D. (Dubois, 149-51). One block is marked no. 1095: i. e., shipment 1095.

[129] In Strabo's time (5, 2, 5) Carrara marble was preferred to all others for public and private structures. This popularity was due, according to him, to the ease of its transport; for Luna was a seaport and the blocks could be sent from the quarries on river barges. Between 22-27 A. D. the quarries became state property and by the time of the Flavians the marble was used so extensively that a special bureau for its reception was established at Rome.

[130] The famous quarries of Mons Claudianus (hornblende granite) were opened by Claudius (Pl., 36, 57), but the period of great use of granites at Rome was during the reigns of Hadrian and Trajan (Fiehn, 2270; Dubois, 49-75; Johnson, 240).

[131] "The structure looked like a raised causeway, fourteen metres wide, protruding into the river for twenty-six metres, at an angle of 40° with the direction of the stream. On each side of the causeway there are spacious landings built of concrete and faced with a palisade." Lanciani, *The Ruins and Excavations of Ancient Rome*, 1897, 525; Dubois, XXXIX.

[132] Marble chips, yellow crystalline sand used for sawing blocks, tools, and unfinished work have been discovered along the Tiber from the Emporium to the Mausoleum of Augustus. Lanciani ("Officina Marmoraria della regione XIII," *B. C.*, XIX [1891], 23-26) locates the *statio* near the wharf in the Campus Martius. See, however, Hülsen's criticism in *Röm. Mitt.*, VII (1892), 322.

Herodes Atticus in the time of Hadrian was apparently the last individual to quarry marble from his estate on Mt. Pentelicus; yet the process by which the state had gained possession of all the most important deposits had been a gradual one.[133] In the last century of the republic, when marble was beginning to be used, wealthy private citizens or returning generals had introduced the new decorative building material at Rome.[134] Cicero (*ad Att.*, 12, 19, 1) gives a hint of the way in which the ordinary individual obtained marble for his projects: when he was interested in procuring columns of Chian marble for Tullia's shrine, he planned to get them from Apella, a native of Chios residing for business purposes at Rome. Perhaps this Jew may be compared with the Bithynian, M. Aurelius Aquila, who had his *statio* (storerooms and offices) in the warehouse of M. Petronius.[135] In either case it is impossible to determine whether these men are agents for larger dealers or independent importers. C. Tullius Crescens, the only *negotiator marmorum* mentioned in the inscriptions (VI, 33886), also had his shop and storeroom in the warehouse district (*de Galbes*). This freedman probably retailed imported marble in small quantities to sculptors or under-contractors in private projects.

The importation of marble from state-owned quarries for public buildings, begun by Caesar, had already assumed considerable proportions during the reign of Augustus. Some indication of the vast amounts imported for later imperial projects can be given by an analysis of the marbles used in the building of Trajan's Forum.

After Apollodorus' plans for the basilica, libraries, temple, and colonnades had been approved, orders for the required

---

[133] Hirschfeld, *Die kaiserlichen Verwaltungsbeamten bis auf Diocletian*, 1905, 146-150, and Dubois, IX-XIII.

[134] Crassus in 92 B. C. had imported six columns of marble from Hymettus (Pl., 36, 7); M. Lepidus in 78 had introduced giallo antico; Mamurra had introduced the custom of veneering walls with Luna marble (*id.*, 36, 48, etc.). During the later years of the Republic Luna marble was used for public buildings (Frank, *An Economic Survey*, I, 370), but none of the markers published by Bruzza and Dubois are earlier than 64 A. D. (the date of the reconstruction of the warehouse).

[135] See Chap. III, n. 7.

marble were sent to the imperial quarries throughout the empire; and soon vessels began to arrive at Ostia carrying the 50,000 tons needed for the pavements, veneered walls, and 900 columns of this project.[136] If merchant vessels of ordinary size had been used, approximately 625 ships carrying the marble for this forum would have docked at Rome's seaport within the period of a few years. Each of the 50 granite columns which outlined the inner nave of the Basilica Ulpia was a monolith, weighing about 38 tons before dressing;[137] these came from the island of Elba.[138] Trajan's column was probably imported in 18 solid cubes (about 4.5 m. on a side before dressing), each weighing about 50 tons. The whole column represented a total import of over 1,000 tons of Parian marble. From Euboea came the columns of cipollino (about 50) in the outer aisle of the basilica, and from Chemtou the material for 16 columns and the steps of the entrance facade. Luna marble and great slabs of pavonazetto were also imported for the pavement and walls of the hall.

Wood. The source of the wood employed in such constructions is difficult to determine. Certainly there was not a plentiful supply close at hand, though the elder Pliny tells of some timber floated down the tributaries of the Tiber and of the dam built in the upper sources to facilitate the traffic.[139] This statement of Pliny, joined to Strabo's account

---

[136] Mau, "Die Inschrift der Trajanssäule," *Röm. Mitt.*, XXII (1907), 189, gives the total at 26,600 cu. m.; Cozzi's total given by Sogliano in *Atti della Reale Accademia di Napoli*, XXV (1908), 90-2, is 25,938 cu. m. Other calculations have been taken from this source.

[137] The great monoliths for imperial buildings were doubtless quarried as rectangular solids and dressed either at the wharves or near the building operations. The central space in Trajan's column, through which the stairway runs, was probably cut after the column had been erected (see Lehmann-Hartleben, *Die Trajanssäule*, 1926, 146, n. 7). Industrial activities resulting from state imports of marble were very great: there is inscriptional evidence for *caesores* (cutters), *politores* (polishers), *lapidarii* (stone-cutters), *marmorarii* (workers in marble), *quadratarii* (hewers of large blocks), etc., engaged in imperial projects.

[138] Ricci, *Via dell'Impero*, 1933, 128; see also Platner-Ashby, 241.

[139] Pl., 3, 53: "The Tiber is at first small and navigable only by means of sluices (*piscinis*) by which the water is impounded and discharged, as is done also in the case of the Tinia and the Clanis, which flow into it; the water is collected for 9 days, unless rain should help. But even then the Tiber, on account of its rugged

of the wooden utensils made at Nuceria (5, 2, 10), suggests that some timber may have come to Rome from Umbria during the early empire. Pisa, however, whose prosperity in the past had been due to the timber it sent to Rome, had become a quiet place in Strabo's day because the wood along the Arno had now been used up.[140] This same condition probably prevailed in the forests of Bruttium, though the state-owned tracts of Sila had generally supplied pitch, not cut wood.[141] From forests in Liguria, however, timber had always been brought in quantities.[142] Later, when records of contracts let by the state for wood to heat the baths become known, wood is coming from other locations outside of Italy: in the fourth century the *mancipes* imported from Africa and Gaul,[143] and possibly these countries had been meeting the needs of the city from a much earlier date.[144] Fine woods, such as boxwood and maple for furniture, were probably imported from the southern coast of the Euxine from Sinope to Bithynia (Str., 12, 3, 12; 12, 3, 10; Pl., 16, 71). Moreover, some of the cedars, spruce, firs, and cypress of Lebanon, on which the state had established a monopoly in the days of Hadrian, were sent to the city ("Libanos," *P.-W.*, XIII[1], 7). Mauretanian citrus wood is discussed later.

---

and uneven channel, is really more suitable for navigation by rafts (*trabibus*) than by boats (*ratibus*) for any distance." These rafts could be used for timber at Rome.

[140] Strabo (5, 2, 5) states that most of the long, straight timber had been used for buildings at Rome or for villas nearby.

[141] Verres, however, hauled timber from Bruttium to Sicily (Cic., *in Verr.*, 5, 47). For an earlier period see *id.*, *Brutus*, 85.

[142] Especially for shipbuilding (Str., 5, 2, 5; cf. *N. S.*, 1914, 113-134).

[143] For Africa see *Cod. Theod.*, 13, 5, 10, with Waltzing's comment (II, 55). The forests of Thabraca were proverbial (see Juv., 10, 194 and *Mélanges d'arch. et d'hist.*, XLVIII [1931], 27). The export of Gallic wood to Ostia for state baths is discussed by Grenier, 579-80 ff. There are numerous inscriptions in Gaul of *lignarii*, *ratiarii*, and even of a *negotiator artis ratiariae*.

[144] The corporation of shippers at Ostia known as the *navicularii lignarii* (XIV, 278) may have been engaged in carrying wood for governmental needs, but until the date of the inscription can be determined there is no way of knowing the guild's function. In the city itself the *porticus inter lignarios* near the Porta Trigemina had been erected in the second century B. C. to serve as shelter for those who traded in wood nearby (Livy, 35, 41, 10), and it is likely that a similar landing place existed in the empire.

IV. METALS

Gold. The mines of Spain were for the imperial treasury a constant and almost inexhaustible source of income, for according to Pliny (3, 30) very nearly the whole peninsula abounded in mines of gold, silver, copper, iron, lead, and tin.[145] Both Pliny (33, 78) and Statius (*Silvae,* 3, 3, 89) testify to the large quantities of unworked gold that came to the capital: in Vespasian's time 20,000 pounds of lump gold were imported annually from the districts of the northwest, preëminently Asturia (Pl., *loc. cit.*). As early as Augustus most of the gold mines had belonged to the state (Str., 3, 2, 10), and under Tiberius even the rich Spanish deposits of the *Montes Mariani* became part of the imperial monopoly.[146] The lines from Statius further imply that by the time of Domitian there was a centralized control of gold mines by the " Chancellor of the Exchequer." Although in the early empire most of the gold sent to Rome came from Spain, Strabo mentions the metal among the exports of Britain (4, 5, 2) and refers to Gallic mines in the Basses-Pyrénées among the Tectosages and the Tarbelli (4, 1, 13; 4, 2, 1). There are other brief notices in the geographer to gold mines among the Ligurian Salassi (4, 6, 7) and among the Noric Taurisci (4, 6, 12), while Pliny tells of a mine in Dalmatia which in Nero's day yielded a daily output of 50 pounds (33, 67).

In the time of Trajan a vast tonnage of gold came to the fiscus from newly conquered Dacia. The Byzantine Lydus declared that 5 million pounds weight of gold and 10 of silver were sent to Rome (*de Magistratibus,* 2, 28); but Carcopino, altering the absurd figures, concludes that 500,000 pounds of gold (2250 million sesterces) were sent from the Transylvanian mines during the period of Roman occupation.[147] Trajan's gigantic public structures and the prodigal

---

[145] See the discussion of Van Nostrand, " Roman Spain," *An Economic Survey,* III, 150-174.

[146] Tac., *Ann.,* 6, 19; Suet., *Tib.,* 49. By Vespasian's time most of the Spanish mines belonged to the fiscus or the patrimonium. One famous exception was the cinnabar mines of Sisapo (Hirschfeld, 149, n. 2).

[147] *Points de vue sur l'impérialisme romain,* 1934, 83-86. The

games described in the Fasti of Ostia resulted from this increase in public revenue.

Silver. Silver was found in almost all the provinces, but Pliny (who had been an imperial procurator in Spain) declared that Spanish silver, with its companion lead, was the finest. The amounts mined during the empire can be inferred only from the finds and records about lead, for the figures from earlier periods do not apply later.[148] In the early principate all Spanish silver mines had been private (Str., 3, 2, 10) and there are records of private workings as late as the Flavian period, but the famous *Lex Metalli Vipascensis* (*C. I. L.,* II, 5181: probably from the time of Vespasian) as well as Pliny's discussion of newly reopened mines (34, 165) postulates state-owned holdings operated by contractors on a 50-50 basis. The silver, separated from the lead at the place of mining, was shipped to the capital for coinage and the arts.[149]

Lead. Source information about the imports of lead from Spain, Britain, and Sardinia can be obtained from the seven billets found at Rome.[150] One billet (*C. I. L.,* XV, 7916) of over 77 pounds, found in the Tiber between the Forum Boarium and the marble wharf (where it had probably fallen overboard during the unloading of a Spanish vessel), had, according to the testimony of its stamp, been obtained as a by-product of silver at the mines of Mt. Ilurco (Baetica). It is interesting to note that the three billets from Britain are of

attacks of Syme (*J. R. S.,* XX [1930], 55 ff.) and of Davies (*Roman Mines in Europe,* 1930, 205) have been adequately answered at 86, n. 1.

[148] In Polybius' time the revenue from Spanish silver mines was 25,000 drachmas daily (Str., 3, 2, 10), and in Hannibal's day the mines of Baebelo yielded 300 lbs. each day (Pl., 33, 97). Imperial writers, however, give no accounts of the richness of Spanish silver mines.

[149] When Caesar made his first entry into the city he found in the aerarium 30,000 lbs. of uncoined silver as well as 15,000 of gold (Pl., 33, 56). The officials of the fiscus would have abundant metal to sell to the Roman silversmiths.

[150] Besnier, "Le commerce du plomb à l'époque romaine," *Revue archéologique,* XIII (1921), 121-7. Of these seven, three originated in Spain, one in Sardinia, and three in Britain (see *C. I. L.,* XV, 7914-20).

a later period than the three Spanish ones, a confirmation of the well-known fact that, after the lead deposits at Mendip began to be worked (as early as 49 A. D.), the ease with which the ore could be obtained soon caused British lead to usurp the market.[151] This cheap lead was in demand for water pipes in the city's extensive system of aqueducts, and attempts have been made to suggest the size of the lead import by determining the weight of a few of the larger pipes.[152] A large pipe line (from the reservoir by Porta Viminalis to the Forum of Trajan) was 1750 meters long and weighed nearly 233 tons, and there were in use, it must be remembered, thousands of lines almost as long.

Iron. Considerable quantities of iron were also needed, but it is not likely that raw material in any bulk came to the city: the mines were distant, freight charges were expensive, and there was not sufficient fuel near Rome to encourage production on a large scale. The mines of Noricum, let out by the fiscus to contractors, sent iron to be made into tools and blades at factories near Comum and Sulmo (Pl., 34, 144-5). References to fine implements of Noric iron are proverbial at Rome; [153] in fact, there was a sales depot (*statio*) in the city maintained by merchants from here (*C. I. L.,* VI, 250). The iron of Elba, however, continued to be mined as in the days of the republic; but instead of being shipped to nearby Populonia, which in Strabo's day had ceased to be a centre of the iron industry (5, 2, 6), the sponges were sent to Puteoli (Diodorus, 5, 13; Pl., 34, 142). Many of the heavier farm and household implements as well as armor of all types came by sea from this city to Rome,[154] but inscriptions of smiths, lock makers, nail makers, and key makers in the capital prove

---

[151] Collingwood, " Roman Britain," *An Economic Survey,* III, 1937, 42-45.
  [152] Lanciani, *The Ruins and Excavations,* 529.
  [153] For example, Hor., *Epod.,* 17, 71; *Carm.,* 1, 16, 9; Ov., *Met.,* 14, 712. The iron of Tarraconensis in Spain, though not equal in purity to that of Noricum, was made into weapons and cutlery for the Roman market at Toletum, Turiasso, and Bilbilis (Pl., 34, 144). Implements from the Pontic Chalybes (Str., 12, 3, 9) would also reach the city.
  [154] The two *negotiatores ferrarii* (VI, 9665-6) probably imported this ware.

that small articles of daily use were made to order.[155] Iron
clamps used to hold together blocks of tufa and travertine,
probably made by Roman smiths, were also in constant demand; it has been calculated that 300 tons were required for
clamps in the Colosseum alone.[156] Furthermore, the beams
that supported the projecting porches of the city's numerous
tenement houses were usually made of iron.

Copper and Bronze. The import of copper and bronze ware
resembled that of iron: individual coppersmiths of the capital
undoubtedly made articles of everyday use, but the greater
part of copper ware came from Capua, the chief centre of
production (Pl., 34, 95). Evidence for the traffic in copper
wine containers, platters, ladles, bowls, and pots, or for bronze
statuary and artistic metal furniture between this city and
Rome is considerable,[157] and the inscription of L. Statius
Onesimus *viae Appiae multorum annorum negotians (C. I. L.,*
VI, 9663) may indicate the route used.[158] On the other hand,
bronze token money continued to be coined at Rome during
the empire, and sculptors of bronze portrait heads undoubtedly
found their wealthiest patrons in the capital. Copper for these
projects came mainly from Spanish mines, either worked directly under imperial procurators or let out to lessees who paid
for their privileges in kind.[159]

V. HOUSEHOLD FURNISHINGS

Pottery. Most of the earthenware used by the tenement
dwellers of Rome was made in the factories at Arretium.
These red bowls and plates (which had begun to be imported

---

[155] See Chap. II, section on Copper and Iron.
[156] Cozzo, 213.
[157] Willers (*Neue Untersuchungen über die römische Bronzeindus-
trie*, 1907, 28). See also *C. I. L.*, XV, 7074-7105 for inscriptions on
articles found at Rome: C. Oppi Herma[e] (7078) and Nas[enni]
Liban[i] (7077) on bronze cooking pots are the trade-marks for
well-known Capuan factories.
[158] This merchant has been identified by Willers (*ibid.*) with the
Statius Onesimus recorded on an inscription at Aquileia (V, 827).
The Statii of Aquileia exported Capuan bronze in large quantities
to northern districts.
[159] For Spanish copper see Str., 3, 2, 8 and Pl., 3, 30. The copper
mines of Cyprus were also imperial property by Augustus' time
(Str., 14, 6, 5; Jos., *Ant.*, 16, 4, 5).

in the last years of the republic) were sent in greater quantities to the capital during the first century A. D. (Mart., 14, 98; Pl., 35, 160), and many of the finds at Rome have been identified as the work of Greek artisans employed in the Etrurian shops.[160] Consignments were probably carried in wagons to Clusium and thence shipped down the Clanis to the Tiber and the wharves of Rome.[161] Later, certainly by the end of the first century, ware from Gallic potteries was to be found in the city; [162] at the same time cheap clay cups from Saguntum were in common use.[163] During all this early period, however, crude clay storage jars and even cheap plates and cups were produced in workshops on the Vatican Hill.[164]

Glass. Though it is generally assumed, on the basis of Strabo's remarks (16, 2, 25), that glass was manufactured at Rome,[165] the mixture of dark volcanic debris in the sand along the Tiber and the Latian coast about Ostia makes the assumption improbable. Lower down the coast at the mouth of the Volturnus, however, the sand was suitable and factories did develop (Pl., 36, 194). Imports from this centre came to the city in some bulk: the work of A. Volumnius Januarius, Caecilius Hermes, and Asinius Philippus, all Campanians, has been found at Rome.[166] Finer crystal demanded by the

---

[160] The inscriptions are recorded in *C. I. L.*, XV, 4925-6063. Some pieces of black ware are listed, but most of the red ware belongs to the early years of Augustus. The chronology of the exports from the shops of the M. Perennii has been recently discussed by Oxé (*Arretinische Reliefgefässe vom Rhein*, 1933). See also Chase, *Catalogue of Arretine Pottery*, 1916, 2-5; 18-27.

[161] Some import from Campania (Mart., 14, 114; 14, 102) and perhaps from Mutina (Pl., 35, 161) must also be considered for this period.

[162] The beginning of the south Gallic industry is discussed by Oxé (*Frühgallische Reliefgefässe vom Rhein*, 1934). Export to Italy before 79 A. D. is proved by the consignments found at Pompeii which had been packed at Rome (Atkinson, *J. R. S.*, IV [1914], 27). There may have been middlemen at the capital who received Gallic ware and distributed it to other Italian towns. Grenier (541 ff.) states that plates from Graufesenque were sent to Italy from the days of Nero, but in small quantities until 75 A. D.

[163] Pl., 35, 160; Mart., 4, 46, 15; 8, 76; 14, 108; 8, 6, 2; Juv., 5, 29.

[164] See Chap. II, 95.

[165] See the discussion of this problem in Chap. II, section on Glassware.

[166] *C. I. L.*, XV, 6970, 6968, and 6960. See Gummerus, "Industrie

rich came from Alexandrian factories [167] and from Phoenicia.[168] There was also a small import from Gaul and Spain after the first century.[169] This glass import included not only goblets and containers of all shapes but mosaics, some glass mirrors, and imitation precious stones.

Furniture. The carpenters of the city, organized into their huge guilds, could easily supply the simple tables and couches used in the poorer households.[170] There is evidence, moreover, of prosperous *fabri tignuarii* at Ostia who may have owned factories of rather large size.[171] The more elaborate furniture, as illustrated by the finds at Pompeii, with hand-carved legs, inlays of ivory, or finely-wrought metal bases, however, required tools and raw materials beyond the reach of these ordinary cabinetmakers.[172] Consequently, it is likely that the guild of *Neapolitani citrarii* (VI, 9258), Neapolitan artisans engaged in making citrus tables inlaid with ivory, exported to the city.[173] Although information about the production of this luxury ware at Rome is very meagre, it is likely that the *negotiatores eborarii et citrarii,* who formed a large guild at Rome in the time of Hadrian (VI, 33885), were also makers of intarsia tables and other expensive furniture.[174]

---

und Handel," *P.-W.*, IX, 1463-6; 1478-9; Kisa, *Das Glas im Altertume*, 1908, 722-5. At Puteoli there was a *clivus vitriarius* (X, 1695).

[167] The import is first mentioned by Cicero (*pro Rab. Post.*, 14, 40). Cedrenus (Migne, *Patrologiae Cursuscomplectus*, 121, 337) tells of a ship from Alexandria which came to Rome in the reign of Augustus laden with glass, paper, and linen. Statius (*Silvae*, 3, 3, 94) names glass from Alexandrian workshops among the products coming to the fiscus (see Rostovtzeff, " Fiscus," *D. E.*, III, 136-7). Martial (12, 74, 1) speaks of crystal from the Nile.

[168] For Syrian glass see *C. I. L.*, XV, 6958; *I. G.*, XIV, p. 707.

[169] Kisa, 938. The Cologne ware was important for the second and third centuries A. D. (Grenier, 625).

[170] See Chap. II, section on Building. The guild in 154 A. D. had 1000-1500 members (VI, 1060).

[171] For manufacturing at Ostia see Frank, " The People of Ostia," *Cl. J.*, XXIX (1934), 485. The Ostian carpenters' guild had 250 members in 198 A. D. (XIV, 4569).

[172] Cf. Richter, *Ancient Furniture*, 1926, 148-158.

[173] One of the most frequently mentioned articles in the *Periplus* is luxury furniture from Arabia and India.

[174] So Waltzing, II, 525; IV, 17. The theory that these guild members were importers operating with extensive capital is incongruous to the details of the inscription. Small retailers of such ware would, moreover, be very unusual.

4

In addition, abundant raw materials for cabinetmakers and specialists in intarsia were available at the capital. According to the famous passage in Statius (*Silvae*, 3, 3, 89-95), Mauretanian citrus wood and African ivory came as some form of tax in kind to the fiscus. This ancient testimony is strengthened by finds of over 675 cu. ft. of ivory (shall we say 2,500 tusks?) in one of the excavated rooms of the Horrea Galbiana.[175] In the second place, there was a great amount of ivory from the elephants slaughtered at the games; it is more than possible that some of the ivory in the fiscal warehouse came from this source.[176] Furthermore, the Sabrathenses, who had a storage and sales depot in the great commercial portico at Ostia, engaged in the independent ivory trade.[177] By the time of Pliny, however, the supply of African ivory had been depleted, and the growing interest in Ethiopian and Indian commerce was motivated, in part at least, by the popular mania for citrus tables with ivory supports: Seneca, who owned over 500 of these tables, was an unusually avid geographer (Dio, 61, 10, 3).[178] Yet the citrus wood tops continued to come from Mauretania during this period (Mart., 9, 22, 5; 12, 66, 6). Ebony for other luxury furniture was brought from Ethiopia (Pl., 12, 17; Str., 17, 2, 2) and tortoise shell, from Ariaca in northwest India (*Periplus*, 6).

VI. LUXURY IMPORTS

The tremendous size of the luxury import in Pliny's day is revealed by his statement (12, 84) that 100,000,000 ses-

---

[175] Lanciani, *Ancient Rome*, 250; also Romanelli, *D. E.*, III, 986.

[176] Pliny (8, 20-22) says that at the dedication of the temple of Venus Victrix in 55 B. C., 18 (or perhaps 20) elephants were killed; in the third consulship of Caesar, 20 were matched against 500 soldiers, etc.

[177] *C. I. L.*, XIV, Suppl., p. 662, no. 14. Sabrata was located at the juncture of a caravan route along which ivory, ostrich feathers, and perhaps gold were brought from the centre of Africa. Romanelli ("Ricordi di Tripolitani a Roma e in Italia," *B. C.*, LVI [1928], 71-2) declares the elephant pictured on the mosaic floor of this depot is clear proof of the interest of these merchants in the ivory trade. In the year 138 A. D. the Sabrathenses at Rome set up an honorary decree to Hadrian's wife (*N. S.*, 1933, 433) in the Forum of Caesar. Paribeni, who published the inscription, suggests that at this period African traders were supplying animals for the royal menagerie.

[178] Pliny (8, 7) speaks of the failure of African ivory; for the explorations of the south of Egypt in Nero's reign see Suet., *Nero*, 31.

terces ($5,000,000) were drained annually from the empire
to India, the Seres, and Arabia.   In another passage (6, 101)
he notes that over one-half of the amount, 55,000,000 sesterces, was absorbed by India, which gave in return merchandise selling for over a hundred times its original cost because
of the expenses of the journey.[179]   These figures, moreover,
are not exaggerated, for Pliny was a member of Vespasian's
cabinet and shared the emperor's concern over the adverse
balance of trade.   A record of the articles included in this
trade and of its expansion in the first half of the first century
is contained in the famous *Periplus* of the Erythraean Sea
written about 60 A.D. by a merchant from Berenice engaged
in carrying Indian luxuries through Egypt.[180]   All of the vessels carrying the wares enumerated in this account did not, of
course, put in at Rome—some went directly to Spain and
Gaul; yet the luxury importations to the city must have far
surpassed those to all the rest of the western world.

Return cargoes from Rome or Latium are never mentioned
in this account, and this absence of exports is further demonstrated by the guilds of stevedores at Ostia engaged in putting
ballast into ships to serve as a make-up load for the return
journey eastward (*C. I. L.*, XIV, 448).[181]

Gems and Pearls. Since a signet ring was required by every
citizen of any importance and, if we can believe Pliny, pearl
earrings or necklaces by their wives, the amount of precious
and semiprecious stones imported by the *gemmarii* and *margaritarii* of Rome must have been enormous.   Pliny's wrath-

---

[179] Pliny (12, 63-5) discusses the cost of bringing a camel's load
of frankincense from Sabatha (Arabia) to Gaza, a distance of about
2,400 English miles. For the entire trip of 65 days the cost was
approximately 688 denarii ($138) per camel; that is, about $2 a
day. As each load weighed about 750 lbs., 75 lbs. were carried for
1 denarius a day; thus for 65 days the portage was nearly 1 denarius
a pound. At Rome the pound of frankincense sold for 3 to 6 denarii.
[180] Schoff, *The Periplus of the Erythraean Sea*, 1912, pp. 7-15. In
sec. 10 the large ships built to carry this luxury trade are mentioned.
Strabo (17, 1, 13) says that in earlier days no more than 20 vessels
a year traversed the Arabian Gulf, but that at his time (Augustus'
reign) large fleets were dispatched to India (see Warmington, *The
Commerce between the Roman Empire and India*, 1928, 35-83).
[181] Warmington (272-318) discusses the adverse balance and concludes that it was not detrimental to the prosperity of the empire.

ful enumeration of the strange and extravagant use of pearls (9, 114) helps to explain the fortunes amassed by some of the urban importers.[182] In addition, the demands of the emperors and the imperial court had always to be considered; on one occasion the wife of Gaius is said to have appeared wearing two million dollars worth of emeralds and pearls (Pl., 9, 17), and Julius Caesar is said to have given Sempronia a pearl worth $30,000 (Suet., *Jul.*, 50).

A few pearls of inferior quality came from the Red Sea, but the Persian Gulf and the Gulf of Manaar (on the west coast of India) were the chief sources of supply.[183] The independent merchant who carried these Eastern luxuries, as exemplified by the author of the *Periplus,* needed ample means to equip his rather large vessel, to secure an out-going cargo, and to provide armed guards; on many occasions, moreover, a stay-at-home capitalist backed the venture.[184] There is no indication that the state supervised or controlled this commerce except the passage in Statius (*Silvae,* 3, 3, 90) which includes pearls among the products coming to the fiscus, and in all probability the notice refers to the revenues (in kind, perhaps) paid by these Indian merchants at the Red Sea ports of Myos Hormos and Berenice.[185]

The evidence afforded by existing Roman jewels coupled with the testimony of Pliny reveals that these Far Eastern cargoes frequently included the highly prized sardonyx, diamonds, agates, sards, carnelians (from which the costly myrrhine goblets were made), emeralds, jaspers, rubies, and beryls.[186] To this list of imports can be added Scythian emer-

---

[182] See Chap. III, section on Jewelry and Metal Work, where the inscriptions of the 17 *margaritarii* known from the city are discussed.
[183] So Pliny, 9, 113; *Periplus*, 19. For a detailed discussion of the location of pearl fisheries see Rommel, " Margaritai," *P.-W.,* XIV², 1687-9, and Warmington, 167-71.
[184] Warmington, 310-11. He also suggests that the state lent money and sent out merchants in connection with state factories in Egypt, but of such activities there is no proof.
[185] The most important of these dues was the *vectigal Maris Rubri* levied on all Arabian, African, and Indian wares that entered Egyptian territory. The collection was let to tax-farmers in Pliny's day (6, 84).
[186] Rossbach, " Gemmen," *P.-W.,* VII, 1088-1113.

alds (Mart., 4, 28; 14, 109), rubies and tourmaline from Egypt and Ethiopia (Pl., 37, 39), and amber from the regions of the Baltic Sea.[187] Since the mines of precious and semi-precious stones of Egypt were a government monopoly, quantities also came from this source.[188]

Wares from Egypt. A great part of the gold and silver drained from the empire to India paid for the spices, drugs, and unguents which, passing through Egyptian ports, were prepared for Roman markets at Alexandria.[189] Because of its wide use as a medicine and as a table spice, pepper was the most important article of trade and formed probably over half of the cargo of ships bound west from Egypt.[190] In the first century of the empire Alexandrian ships carrying this spice usually landed at Puteoli, and the large sacks were brought by wagon to the merchants on the Vicus Tuscus and later to the Horrea Piperataria on the Sacred Way.[191] To this same market came the other precious plant products enumerated in Pliny's twelfth book: Gallic nard, balsam from Judea, frankincense and myrrh from Arabia, ginger and cinnamon carried by the Arabians, casia carried by the Somali, and spikenard and malabathrum from India.[192] In Trajan's day whole cinnamon trees were sent through Ostia to the horrea for storage (Galen, XIV, 64 and 79, K.). Enormous quantities of perfumes, made from roses and olive oil, also came

---

[187] Julianus, the procurator of Nero, brought back such quantities from the Baltic that nets, arms, and litters in the amphitheatre were decorated with it (Pl., 37, 42, and 45). According to Pliny, some amber came to Rome in a raw state, though most of it was worked at Aquileia.

[188] Johnson, 241 and 326.

[189] Pliny (12, 59) describes the care taken in supervising the preparation of frankincense in these factories. The passage intimates large-scale production requiring capital; perhaps there is a suggestion of government interest (Johnson, 340; Warmington, 310).

[190] Warmington, 182. On the Digest list of wares subject to duty on entering Egyptian ports from the Red Sea, pepper does not appear, probably a concession to the common people at Rome.

[191] See Chap. III, section on the Horrea Piperataria.

[192] Schmidt, *Drogen und Drogenhandel im Altertum*, diss. Köln, 1924. Pliny (12, 83) tells us that at Poppaea's funeral Nero used up more spices than came from Arabia in a year. See also Juvenal (4, 108; 8, 159) on the extravagant use of amomum (from Media and Armenia) for burials.

to the city from Capua, where large producers made up goods that won wide renown.[193]

The assumption is not unwarranted that some of the consignments of Eastern spices and ointments were directed to state shops and manufactories in Egypt. That the Romans had continued the Ptolemaic monopoly in this branch of industry is unlikely, for concessions to individual producers and dealers are revealed by numerous papyri. Egypt, however, had always stood in a peculiar relationship to the head of the Roman state, and the policy of tribute in kind which appears fully organized in the *anabolica* of the third century may have had its roots back in an earlier period.[194] Accord-

---

[193] These were sold in a district called the Seplasia (Philipp, " Seplasia," *P.-W.*, IV, Zweite Reihe, 1546). Pliny (18, 111) says Campania produced more unguents than other countries oil.

[194] The nature and extent of the tribute in kind exacted by Rome from the provinces of the empire are defined by scant evidence; and it is often assumed that wheat, and occasionally other grains, were the only *natura* exported to the centre of government. To be sure, requisitions of clothing, food, and transport animals for armies operating in the provinces had been made from earliest times, and the state had never hesitated to exact supplies for visiting officials. Later these sporadic requisitions, primarily for military needs, were regularized into an annual tax (*anabolica*). For Egypt, at least, there are clear records of shipments of linen, glass, paper, and spices sent to the state warehouses along the Tiber (Vopiscus, *Aur.*, 45). This literary evidence for the time of Aurelian rather indicates than precludes an earlier organization, probably during the reigns of the Severi or the late Antonines. Moreover, there is every reason to believe that the principle of *natura* was always recognized by the Roman government, when it so desired (cf. the silphium from Cyrene, Pl.,´19, 40).

The problems connected with the shipments of such taxes to Rome and the subsequent intervention of the agencies of the fiscus in their distribution have been treated fully for grain alone. Less details are known about the 50 per cent tax in kind exacted from lessees of imperial mines and the blocks of marble and granite shipped by procurators to fiscal offices at Rome. In addition, the famous passage from Statius apparently enumerated produce in kind which came to the fiscal official *a rationibus* in the time of Domitian (*Silvae*, 3, 3, 89 ff.).

It is generally agreed that the following items are listed, though there is some variety in the interpretation of any single one: Spanish and Dalmatian gold, African and Egyptian grain, pearls from Eastern seas, wool from Tarentum, glass, citrus wood from Africa, and Indian ivory. The wool may have come to the patrimonium from imperial estates around Tarentum, the glass as tax from the factories in Alexandria, and the pearls, ivory, and wood from duties exacted on the empire's boundaries. There is no proof that such duties were exacted in kind, but the possibility exists. Statius'

ingly, discussion of exports from Egypt must always consider this possibility. Linen, papyrus, and crystal from Alexandrian workshops belong to this group.[195]

Animals for the Games. An import of considerable bulk that came with regularity to the urban docks were animals for the games at Rome. According to Dio (68, 15) Trajan in the year 107 A. D. gave shows for 123 days in which 11,000 animals were killed. That this figure is not grossly exaggerated can be demonstrated by comparison with the prodigalities recorded in the *Fasti Ostienses.*[196] Other figures are available in Pliny,[197] Suetonius (*Claud.*, 21), and the authors of the *Historia Augusta.*[198] These animals came from all parts of the world: camels from Syria, elephants, panthers, and lions from Libya, tigers from India, and race horses from Africa and Spain.[199]

VII. *Stationes*

With the increase of Eastern trade organized groups of merchants and agents of the exporting cities began to appear in the capital. The function of the *stationes* maintained at Rome by traders from Sardis, Tyre, or Palmyra can only be determined by analogy with earlier groups at Puteoli, for the urban inscriptions in general record nothing but the name of the exporting city and of the permanent official, the *stationarius.* On one very important inscription, however (*I. G.,* XIV, 830),[200] it is stated that the agency of the Tyrians in

poetic description cannot be pressed, however, for exact details; the official discussed supervised not only fiscal taxes but also the imperial patrimony and luxuries destined for the emperor's court.

[195] State interest in the products from Egyptian factories is discussed in Chap. III, sections on the Horrea Piperataria and on the Book Trade.

[196] Calza, *N. S.*, 1932, 188-202.

[197] 8, 20: 20 elephants slaughtered; 8, 64: 410 panthers sent to Rome by Pompey, 420 by Augustus; 8, 53: 600 lions exhibited by Pompey, 400 by Caesar, etc.

[198] *Vita Probi*, 19, 7: leopards slaughtered, 100 at a time; *Vita Had.*, 19, 5: 100 lionesses and 300 bears.

[199] Of the horses and their drivers enumerated in *C. I. L.*, VI, 10056, 91 are African and 33 Spanish; in VI, 33937 (= 10053) there are 60 African, 3 Spanish, and 15 others.

[200] The inscription is in the form of a letter written on July 23, 179 A. D., by the Tyrians at Puteoli to the mother city; in it they

Rome is supported by contributions paid by Tyrian ship-masters and importers (*navicularii et mercatores*). Although comparison with the Venetian quarters at Constantinople and with the famous Fondaco dei Tedeschi of the Hansa towns at Venice has been suggested,[201] at Rome there are no indications of a special " quarter " where citizens of the Eastern cities lived grouped together or even of special warehouses by the river. The inscriptions, with slight exceptions, have been found in the western part of the Forum Romanum between the temple of Concord and Caesar's Forum, at the very spot where, in the time of Vespasian, Pliny had located the *stationes municipiorum* (16, 236).[202] Situated at the heart of the capital, the stations could readily be used as exchange houses for large commercial deals or as central reference bureaus for foreign merchants residing in the city. Moreover, whether the agency was a separate building or a section in a larger warehouse, retail shops would be available along the street front. There can be little doubt, however, that with the shifting of the trade to Rome, the warehouses and docks—if not the cemeteries and temples—known from the Tyrian station at Puteoli reappeared at Ostia, or less probably, in the emporium district; and then, after their own reception docks had been erected, the Roman merchants ceased to contribute their share of the rent at Puteoli.

The contribution of about $20,000 made by the Roman branch to the Tyrian agency at Puteoli (*I. G.*, XIV, 830) is a valuable indication of the size of the export trade from Tyre in the second century of the empire. The establishment of a good harbor at Ostia and the decline of Campanian production had finally brought the Eastern ships directly to Rome; but even in the last century of the republic and in the

---

complain that their agency, formerly so wealthy and influential, has become so small that they are unable to pay the rent. These difficulties are increased by the failure of their sister *statio* at Rome to contribute the annual 100,000 denarii ($20,000) which helped to meet their expenses. For a fuller commentary see Dubois, *Pouzzoles antique*, 1907, 83-8.

[201] Cantarelli, " Le *Stationes Municipiorum*," *B. C.*, XXVIII (1900), 124-134, especially 131.

[202] Cantarelli, 127; also De Ruggiero, *Il Foro Romano*, 1913, 51-3.

early first century of the empire, the days of Puteoli's prosperity, the capital had always offered the chief market for luxury articles. Perhaps it is possible to determine the most important of these from the inscriptions naming the cities which established such factories at Rome. First, there was Tyre; and Tyrian ships were generally laden with linen, silk (Chinese, reworked in Syria), glass, and cloth dyed in the famous purple.[203] To the depot maintained by merchants from Sardes (*I. G.,* XIV, 1008-9) came vessels laden with fine cloth, golden jewelry from Lydia, and precious stones.[204] Palmyra transshipped to its western agency the ointments, spices, nuts, woven cloth, and other luxury items enumerated on her famous tariff lists.[205] The merchants from Claudiopolis [206] imported rare silks and myrrhine vessels obtained from the East through Parthian intermediaries; and the city of Tiberias in Galilee [207] sent ships laden with the renowned fish pickle and the dried fruits of the surrounding country. To the depot maintained by Tarsus (*I. G.,* XIV, 1066 a, b) came its excellent tent cloth and cloaks of goat hair, the *cilicum* of Martial. In contrast to these Eastern cities,[208] only one

---

[203] West, " Commercial Syria under the Roman Empire," *Transact. Amer. Philol. Assoc.,* LV (1924), 159-189, especially 169. The weaving of linen assumed enormous proportions along the Syrian coast with the chief centres at Laodiceia and Byblus. At Tyre and Berytus, too, linen was woven, and some silk, though the more common practice was to dye the transparent Chinese materials, and to make them lighter by the drawing of additional threads. The dye works at Tyre were world-famous (Pl., 5, 76; Str., 16, 2, 23). Records of Syrian traders at Rome and Ostia are numerous: *I. G.,* XIV, 830; 1462; *C. I. L.,* VI, 406, etc.

[204] The famous Lydian and Phrygian embroideries had interwoven gold threads like the Attalid tapestries (Pl., 37, 12; 8, 196; 33, 63; etc.).

[205] The record for the *statio* is usually given as *C. I. L.,* VI, 710. Pârvan, however (*Die Nationalität der Kaufläute im römischen Kaiserreich,* 1909, 116-117), does not believe that this dedication indicates an agency and notes other altars set up to Palmyrene gods by private citizens. The tariff-lists have been recently discussed by Heichelheim (" Roman Syria," *An Economic Survey,* IV, 250 ff.).

[206] *C. I. L.,* VI, 342 (= 30742).

[207] Kubitschek, *Jahresheft des österr. arch. Inst.,* VI (1903), 80. See also Hülsen, *Röm. Mitt.,* XX (1905), 9-10 and Gatti, *B. C.,* XXVII (1899), 241-2.

[208] In addition to the agencies named in these chance inscriptions there must have been many others at Rome as well as at Ostia and

district of the West—the district of Noricum—is known to
have established an agency at Rome. This suggests an extensive trade in the fine iron ware from the north as well as in
the goods transshipped through Aquileia.[209]
There is such scanty knowledge about the commerce of the
Roman world that any hints concerning the rather advanced
stage of shipping represented by these stations are highly
valuable. At Rome, as at Puteoli, were the *stationarii,* who
lived in the importing cities and acted as partners or agents
for the exporters in the East.[210] It is likely that these agents
not only received and stored the cargoes in special warehouses
at Ostia but supervised barging the wares up the Tiber and
even displaying them in the Forum booths. Probably some
of the cargo was sold directly to the larger Roman shopkeepers
who went themselves to the warehouses. As a general rule
this system dispenses with the middleman, but the size and
complexity of the trade at Rome and the usual absence of
jobbers in western economy may have caused his emergence.
Of this we have no information.

In contrast to the tremendous size and variety of the import trade, the machinery of transportation has been found to
be poorly developed. The carriers of luxury wares represented by the author of the *Periplus,* the merchants of grain
designated in the Claudian decree, and the importer of wine
exemplified by Petronius, were traders who owned their vessels.[211] It is even probable that the first of these served
both as master of the vessel and managing agent, personally
conducting the sale of his cargo in the open-air markets by the
river. Much of the trade in fruits and vegetables was un-

Portus: a station maintained by Gaza is named in a third century
inscription from Portus (*I. G.,* XIV, 926).

[209] The articles are discussed by Brogan, "Trade between the
Roman Empire and the Free Germans," *J. R. S.,* XXV (1936), 195-
222.

[210] Powerful mercantile companies, formed of numerous stock-
holders, maintained such clerks at branch offices. Dubois (*Pouz-
zoles ant.,* 90) calls them *entrepreneurs et magasiniers* and compares
them to the ἐγδοχεῖς at Delos.

[211] Such merchants who owned one ship, travelling and buying for
themselves, are pictured by Cicero (*in Verr.,* 5, 149). One shipper,
Flavius Zeuxis of Hierapolis, made the trip from Phrygia to Rome
72 times (see Rostovtzeff, 198, n. 30).

doubtedly carried on in this way. It is clear, however, from passages in the earlier jurists that more developed systems were in use in the first centuries of the empire, in which the owner of the vessel employed a shipmaster who in turn " rented space " to exporting merchants.[212] Finally, under the influence of state insurance and encouragement to shippers from the grain provinces, regular schedules (as far as they could be regular in the case of sailing vessels going at the mercy of the weather) were established. And yet because of the regulations of Roman law on *societas*, organized companies of shippers did not come into existence; the several shippers that are named together on the wine or oil sherds from Monte Testaccio are individuals but slightly limited by their union. [213] Though it is quite possible that the middlemen of antiquity are hidden under the simple designation of *vinarius* and *unguentarius*, in general the shipper was very close to the consumer: in the warehouse district around the Galbiana or in the Forum Holitorium the retailer, the consumer, and the ships-captain often met face to face.

---

[212] According to Horace's friend Labeo (*Dig.*, 19, 5, 1, 1) there were two ways available for getting goods transported: 1) to hire a boat, or 2) to contract to have goods carried. The importation of state grain was let out at public auction (Col., 1, praef. 20).

[213] Buckland, *A Text-book of Roman Law from Augustus to Justinian*, 1921, 504-512.

CHAPTER II

INDUSTRY

The essential problem to be considered in this discussion of the industry of Rome is the degree of its similarity with the system of Pompeii, well known because of the abundance of the remains and commonly regarded as typical of the Roman world. Artisan and retail sales booths met the needs of that conservative town with its 25,000 inhabitants lodged in their outspread atrium houses. Rome, on the other hand, supported a population of a million, crowded together in tenement houses that rose to the height of six or seven stories. It is true, of course, that most of the demands of this population were met by imported manufactured ware; as centre of the imperial administration, however, Rome received valuable raw materials that gave rise to some production, and other cheap and bulky raw materials were available close by. For such industries that did develop, then, it may be that large-scale methods emerged to meet the needs of a more complex city life.

I. INNOVATIONS IN DOMESTIC ARCHITECTURE

In no single aspect was the contrast between the two cities greater than in domestic architecture. In picturing imperial Rome one must not think of the familiar atrium houses of Pompeii, but of the tenements of the contemporary harbor town of Ostia: the solid brick construction, the facade of many stories, the ground floor shops with tiny living quarters above, the separate stairways leading from the street to the upper apartments, the overhanging balconies, and the fronting porticoes.[1] This change in domestic architecture car-

---

[1] This discussion of domestic architecture at Rome is based primarily on the following material: Boëthius, " Das Rom der Caesaren," *Die Antike*, XI (1935), 110-138; *id.*, " Das Stadtbild im spätrepublikanischen Rom," *Opuscula Archaeologica*, I, 2, 1935, 179-215; *id.*, " Remarks on the Development of Domestic Architecture at Rome," *A.J.A.*, XXXVIII (1934), 158-170; *id.*, " The Neronian 'Nova Urbs,'" *Corolla Archaeologica*, 1932, 84-97; Harsh, " The

ries with it some implications of change in industrial life. The hypothesis has been suggested that as the Pompeian atrium house was a factor conditioning the development of the small artisan and retail sales shop, these lofty *insulae* may have lead to the appearance of large group manufactories.[2] Though the evidence in support of this theory is meagre, it requires consideration.

The architecture of the capital, designed to offer tradesmen and craftsmen the greatest possible number of shops and lodgings on the street, had its origin in the buildings with *tabernae* erected on either side of the Forum Romanum as early as the fourth century B. C. By the Gracchan period shophouses had appeared in considerable numbers in the district from the Forum to the Velabrum until finally, in the second century A. D., they had almost completely supplanted the atrium house throughout the entire city;[3] they were even making their way into the more conservative life of Pompeii at the time of its destruction.[4] And yet when we see the capital pictured on the Marble Plan of 200 A. D.,[5] the first generalization that is forced on the mind is the frequency with which the small " Pompeian " shop appears. In such vast structures as Trajan's Mercato where, if anywhere, the large shop would be expected to develop, row after row of small booths has been found.[6] In only one respect is there diversity in type: in some shops the artisans worked and lived; in others the living quarters were in a vaulted upper chamber reached by an interior staircase.

Origins of the Insulae at Ostia," *Memoirs of the American Academy in Rome*, XII (1935), 7-66; Van Buren, *Ancient Rome as Revealed by Recent Discoveries*, 1936, 133-40; Lehmann-Hartleben, " Städtebau," *P.-W.*, Zweite Reihe, 2053-65; Wilson, " Studies in the Social and Economic History of Ostia," *Papers of the British School at Rome*, XIII (1935), 41-68.

[2] Rostovtzeff, *Storia economica e sociale*, 1933, 80-81, especially n. 34.

[3] Boëthius, *A. J. A.*, 163. In the fourth century A. D. the population of Rome was lodged in 46,602 of these tenements and 1,790 atrium houses (Fiechter, " Insula," *P.-W.*, IX, 1593).

[4] Carrington, *Pompeii*, 1936, 66-8; 74.

[5] *Forma Urbis Romae Regionum XIIII*, ed. Kiepert and Hülsen, 1896.

[6] Boëthius, *Cor. Arch.*, 90; also *Die Antike*, 126. Ricci, *Via dell'Impero*, 115-20.

There are, however, certain variations in the size and arrangement of these tenement houses which may have bearing on problems of industry and distribution. On the basis of the Marble Plan the Roman houses have been grouped into four classes.[7] The simplest type, the facade structure familiar from the Cardo at Ostia, appears on over twenty fragments as a single row of rather small shops backed by a brick wall.[8] In the second type, exemplified by the Thermae Antoninianae at Pompeii, two houses of the first class are placed back to back along a party wall, but at times they show on the Plan a central court which can be reached through the shops; in most cases this court is probably nothing but a light well.[9] The shops on the ground floor of houses of these first two types are sheltered by the projecting balconies of the second floor, supported by a line of columns. Protection of this nature enabled the merchant, emerging from the confines of his booth, to expose his wares and carry on his trade on the sidewalk.

The more complex tenements of the third and fourth classes are constructed around an inner court. The house above which was built the Church of S. Anastasia,[10] a portion of the Horrea Agrippiana (fr. 37), and the Casa del Larario at Ostia belong to the third group. In many cases, as in the Horrea and in fragments 51 and 86 of the Plan, there is apparently no passage between the shops and the inner area, but when such passages do appear,[11] either through the shops or directly from the streets, we are confronted with a prob-

---

[7] Boëthius, *Opus. Arch.*, 169-171.

[8] Samples are fragments nos. 11, 109c, 138, 149, 170, 199, etc. (the shops in 170 appear unusually long).

[9] An opening into the shops can be seen on fragments 9 and 18. In fragment 287 the larger shops at the end of the house have been separated into smaller units. See also 60, 104, 188, etc.

[10] This structure is discussed by Whitehead, "The Church of S. Anastasia in Rome," *A. J. A.*, XXI (1927), 405-420. The original brown tufa building was contemporary with the Horrea Agrippiana and probably served the same function. In the middle of the first century an extensive series of large rooms (5 x 12 m.) was built to serve as warerooms, or possibly shops; these rooms, however, preserve the essential features of the individualized shop.

[11] Entrances to the shops may be seen on fragments 169, 178, and 109b and c. In the last fragment the entrances are wide and suggest that the court may have been used as a bazaar.

lem. Did the court serve as a bazaar open to the public like the Turkish *khan,* as a warehouse, or possibly as a large workroom? The Plan gives no answer. The same problem arises in connection with houses of the fourth type: the great blocks of the Casa di Diana or the Horrea Epagathiana at Ostia and the *insula* under the Via Nazionale at Rome. This building, dated by the brick stamps before the middle of the second century A. D., was constructed in three parallel sections, each 58.3 x 12 m. The ten or more shops in each section had reached an unusual size, but the persistence of the small vaulted room above them and the lack of communication between the units point to the standardized type of individual enterprise.[12]

Such classification is all that is possible from the remains at hand, and the influence of the changed style of domestic architecture on methods of work continues to be a hypothesis. It is a hypothesis, moreover, which fails to consider that the emergence of production on a large scale depends on many additional factors: labor-saving machinery, cheap fuel, the nearness of essential raw materials, and the interest of the capitalist class in industrial enterprise. Rome had none of these.

II. SCALE OF PRODUCTION

There are three other general considerations which indicate rather definitely the scale of production. That the inhabitants of the capital, like those of Pompeii, preferred articles made to order in small booths is shown in the first place by the very large number of independent craftsmen whose names appear on Roman tombstones.[13] This is not

---

[12] Described by Harsh, 60. The shops in each of the three units extended the width of the entire section and had doors opening on either side to the adjacent ones. According to measurements of the remains the tenement was probably six stories high, the tallest yet excavated.

[13] Records of these are preserved in *C. I. L.*, VI and include such specialists as *aerarii vascularii* (makers of bronze ware, 9138), *anularii* (ring makers, 9144), *argentarii* (silversmiths, 9183-5), *aurifices* (goldsmiths, 9202-8), *caelatores* (engravers of silver plate, 9221), *candelabrarii* (makers of lamp stands, 9228), *centonarii* (makers of patch-work clothes and blankets, 9254), *fabri eborarii* (workers in ivory, 9397), *gemmarii* (stone-cutters, 9433-7), *tibiarii* (flute makers, 9935), etc.

positive proof that great factories employing many slaves did not exist, for slave names, unless preserved on articles of trade, have rarely survived.[14] On the other hand, it may be said that if large metal foundries or shoe factories had been in operation at Rome, there would hardly be records of small artisans in such great quantities. Their very number argues against crushing factory competition.

A second and more convincing proof is furnished by the records of over forty guilds of professional craftsmen in the city.[15] Even this number is, of course, very far from complete, for the organizations are mentioned only casually on inscriptions. Some idea of the enormous quantity of inscriptions that must have been lost may be inferred from the fact that the record of only one—the most important one, to be sure—of the 300 slipper makers at Rome has been preserved.[16] The existence of such artisan groups as we have, however, is contrary to any theory of slave-operated factories. Slaves in factories, although at times they belong to funerary groups, are seldom members of such professional *collegia*.

In the third place, an unusually large number of streets and districts in Rome bore the name of some industry. In medieval times it was the custom for men of a particular occupation to live together in the same quarter, almost monopolizing particular streets and localities: a practice indicated by the street names of older towns. So in Rome the names of Shoemakers Street, Glass Street, and Harness Makers Street probably indicate concentration of individual artisans.[17] At

---

[14] At Patavium, where large woolen mills are known to have been located (Str., 5, 1, 7), there are no epigraphical records of the slave weavers.

[15] The inscriptions of approximately 167 urban guilds, collected by Waltzing (IV, 1-48), include many groups of retail traders. Among the artisan groups, however, are the *anularii* (ring makers, 9144), *aurifices* (goldsmiths, 9202), *brattiarii inauratores* (gilders, 95), *centonarii* (makers of patch-work clothes and blankets, 7861-4), *fabri ferrarii* (ironsmiths, 1892), *fabri tignuarii* (builders, 9034, 996, etc.), *pistores* (bakers, 1002), *plumarii* (embroiderers, 9813), *artifices artis tessalariae lusoriae* (makers of dice for gaming, 9927), etc.

[16] In VI, 9404, the *collegium fabrum soliarium baxiarium* has three " centuries " of members.

[17] Vicus Lorarius (the street of the harness makers; known from one inscription, VI, 9796, found on the Via Appia), Vicus Sandalia-

least, if the location of a home could be designated as *inter falcarios* (Cic., *Cat.*, 1, 8), it is likely that there were no scythe factories in operation at the time. These general considerations have suggested that the small shop system existed and probably prevailed at Rome. Whether this method of work dominated in the specific industries can be determined only by a more detailed investigation.

III. BAKING

In baking there was need for a much larger type of workroom than that offered by the normal shop. The peristyle of the rambling houses at Pompeii had been spacious enough for the operations of such bakeries as that of Region VI, 3, 3, where there have been found four mills turned by horses, storerooms, and a special kneading room.[18] For Rome no remains comparable to these have been found, but in their absence the monument of M. Vergilius Eurysaces near the Porta Maggiore may be used to gain information about bread making on a large scale in the capital.[19] Eurysaces was proud to remind the passerby of his trade by the form of his monument, the inscriptions, and its decorative terra cotta basreliefs. On these reliefs five stages in the work of Eurysaces' bakery are illustrated: cleaning and sieving the grain, grinding (by horses, in this large mill),[20] rolling, baking, and de-

rius (the street of the sandal makers; the street may have received its name from the statue of Apollo Sandaliarius placed there by Augustus: see Platner-Ashby, 577), Vicus Materiarius (the street of the carpenters; VI, 975, near the warehouse district), Scalae Anulariae (the stairs of the ring makers; Suet., *Aug.*, 72), Vicus Vitrarius (the street of the glass blowers; *Not. Reg.* I; see *B. C.*, XLI [1914], 344), Vicus ...ionum Ferrariarum (the street of the smiths; VI, 9185), Vicus Turarius (the street of the perfumers; Hor., *Ep.*, 1, 20, 1 and Porphyrio, *ad loc.*), Vicus Unguentarius (the street of the perfumers; *Not. Reg.* VIII), Sigillaria (the district of the makers of clay statuettes; Col., 2, 3, 5), etc.

[18] Mau, *Pompeii in Leben und Kunst*, 1908, 407-11.

[19] Published in Blümner, *Technologie und Terminologie der Gewerbe und Künste bei Griechen und Römern*, I, 1912, 40 ff. See also the sarcophagus in the Villa Medici (*ibid.*, 40) and the relief from the Museo Chiaramonti (41).

[20] The *pistrinensia iumenta* (animals from the bakeries) seized by Gaius resulted in scarcity of bread at Rome (Suet., *Gaius*, 39). This condition suggests rather large establishments. Water-mills began to be known at Rome in the early empire (Blümner, 47), but were not used to any extent until the fourth and fifth centuries.

5

livery of the loaves to the magistrates. In the relief that shows the kneading process there are two tables at which eight men are at work under the direction of an overseer and, more remarkable, a kneading machine turned by a donkey. From such evidence it can be seen that Eurysaces was no small baker. As his title of *pistor redemptor* implies (*C. I. L.*, VI, 1958), he worked under contract either to supply bread for public slaves and the soldiers stationed near the city, or to meet the needs of many smaller retailers. This large business concern "with scores, perhaps hundreds of working men " [21] was located, we may suppose, in a traditional atrium house or in the court of one of the more complex *insulae*. At Ostia, too, the bakery was housed in a vast single-storied house with an area of about 950 square meters.[22] A wholesale bakery of like size at Rome was probably owned by M. Junius Pudens, the *pistor magnarius pepsianus* (VI, 9810: on a large marble tablet).[23]

The question naturally arises whether bakers with such workrooms dominated the industry at Rome. Fortunately, information about the size of production in the early second century is given by the edict of Trajan offering special privileges to those who milled (for bakers also did the milling) 75 bushels a day.[24] Additional exemptions were extended to those who baked 25 bushels. Since about 70 loaves of bread

---

[21] Rostovtzeff, *Storia econ.*, facing 37.

[22] In this vast mill, the first complete building of the type excavated at Ostia, have been found instruments for grinding, kneading, and cooking; in rooms 6 and 7, for example, were traces of two enormous ovens, and in room 5, numerous millstones (*N. S.*, 1915, 242-9). Calza (244-5) compares the establishment to that of Eurysaces and suggests that the concern was run by a company of bakers. Among the reliefs from the Isola Sacra there is also a mill with a paved floor for the horses (*N. S.*, 1931, 538; see also Boëthius, *Die Antike*, 131-2).

[23] The other *pistor magnarius* (VI, 9811) belongs to the fourth or fifth century, at which time *magnarius* meant the contractor who furnished bread for the gratuitous distributions of the state. (See Mau, " Backerei," *P.-W.*, II, 2736-2742; Waltzing, II, 79-86.) Perhaps Pudens was also a member of this group.

[24] Gaius, 1, 34: *Denique Traianus constituit ut si Latinus in urbe triennio pistrinum exercuerit (quod in) dies singulos non minus quam centenos modios frumenti pinseret ad jus Quiritum*, etc. *Frag. Vat.* 233 (Ulpian) gives further exemptions offered by Hadrian. See also Waltzing, II, 79.

could be made from a bushel of the finest flour (Pl., 18, 89-90) [25] a daily output of about 1,800 loaves may be assumed. When we consider, however, that the state had offered special inducements to encourage work on this scale, the average establishment could not have been very large: the slow and laborious method of baking inevitably checked the size of production.[26] Furthermore, there is every reason to believe that the ancient housekeeper, like the modern one, had no desire to travel along dangerously congested streets any farther than the corner bakeshop.[27] By the fourth century when, instead of wheat, bread was doled out to the citizens, there were from 15 to 24 small public bakeries in each urban region, with a total of 254 for the city.[28]

Since the year 168 B. C. professional bakers had been catering to the wants of the poorer classes (Pl., 18, 107), for the small apartments of the tenement houses had neither the equipment nor the space for home production. In addition, wood was very dear. There is abundant evidence, however, that in the wealthy households the making of bread continued to be a part of home economy during the early empire: in the household of Statilius Taurus, for example, there was an entire guild of bakers (*C. I. L.*, VI, 6219), and in the *familia* of Augustus a freedman spent his time supervising the baking corps (VI, 8998).[29] The imperial freedman who called him-

[25] The reading of Mayhoff (Teubner, 1892: *panis vero e modio similaginis p. XXII e floris modio p. XVI*) substitutes *p.* for the impossible C of some of the manuscripts. Pliny further states that a modius of African wheat yields half a modius of fine flour and 5 sextarii of pollen.

[26] See Blümner, 89-96 and the discussion by T. Warscher, " Breadmaking in Old Pompeii," *Art and Archaeology*, XXX (1930), 103-112.

[27] Labeo (*Jurisprudentiae Antehadrianae*, ed. Bremer, II[1], 85, no. 5) speaks of an *institor* of a baker sent each day to sell bread on a certain street corner in the city; see also Martial, 14, 223. These hawkers, of course, would relieve the delivery problem.

[28] The *Notitia*, in Richter, *Topographie der Stadt Rom*, 1901 (III, 3[2], in Müller's *Handbuch der klassischen Altertumswissenschaft*), 389.

[29] Hirschfeld (*Verwaltungs.*, 243, n. 2) suggests that this freedman, *qui praeest pistoribus*, is supervisor of the bakers who received privileges from the state; the inscription, however, belongs to the period before Trajan. Bakers in various branches of the imperial household are recorded in *C. I. L.*, VI, 4010-12, 4356, 9001 and 9002. Those in large private households are mentioned in 6337-8, 6687, and 9462a. Horace's friend, the lawyer Trebatius, considered that when

self *pistor candidarius* (maker of fine white bread: *C. I. L.*, XIV, 2302: 11 A. D.) had probably learned his trade as a slave on the emperor's staff before he set up his independent shop. The other bakers whose names have survived, with the possible exception of M. Livius Faustus (VI, 9806), were also of servile origin, but their singularly uninstructive inscriptions offer no other information.

There is no definite proof of the existence of a bakers' guild at Rome before the time of Trajan, but his dealings with the group as such implies a previous organization.[30] Later (144 A. D.), in return for additional privileges from the state, we may suppose, the *corpus* of bakers honored Antoninus Pius with a large marble monument (VI, 1002).[31] Since the prefect of the annona is named on the monument and the relief shows a modius filled with grain, it is possible that special terms of buying wheat from the state warehouses had been granted to the guild. Later, when the *collegium* had come under the control of the state, the *mensores* of the granaries at Ostia sold at a low price 200,000 modii to the bakers each month.[32] This wheat was to be used in the making of bread for citizens who still had to buy; wheat for the bread dole was, of course, given to the bakers outright.[33] The nature of any

a home was left by will it included the slave baker, barber, spinning maids, etc. (*Dig.*, 33, 7, 12, 5). Cicero, ridiculing the niggardliness of Piso, declared *pistor domi nullus, nulla cella* (*in Pisonem*, 67).

[30] Aurelius Victor, *de Caesaribus*, 13, 5: *reperto firmatoque pistorum collegio.* Hirschfeld ("Die Getraideverwaltung in der röm. Kaiserzeit," *Philologus*, XXIX [1870], 44) alters *reperto* to *reparato.* Waltzing (II, 79) also declares that Trajan did not establish the guild but joined it with the bureau in charge of the annona.

[31] The high officials of the guild who were in charge of erecting the monument were obviously freedmen: M. Caerellius Zmaragdus and L. Salvius Epictetus.

[32] *Cod. Theod.*, 14, 15, 1 (364 A. D.). Pius and Trajan had revived the bakers' guild by grants of special rights to individual members; the extension of governmental interest in the third century is obscure, although the work of Alexander Severus (222-35 A. D.) in attempting to set in order the food supply of the city probably brought the *collegium pistorum* directly into the employment of the state. By the middle of the fourth century the members, bound by law to their guild, were completely in the power of the government (Kornemann, "Collegium," *P.-W.*, IV, 450-1).

[33] In the later period the Forum Pistorum, mentioned in the Regionary Catalogue for the district of the horrea (Richter, 374), became the centre of production and distribution.

earlier concessions on the part of the government to the guild, however, rests almost entirely on analogy. The absence of records of small independent bakers and the expense of fuel and equipment combine to emphasize the positive evidence of Trajan's edict. Bread retailed in numerous smaller shops was probably, to a large extent, made in bakeries of the size suggested there.

IV. CLOTHING

We have seen that much finished clothing was imported to the city in the form of tunics from Canusium or cloaks from Gaul. Woolen cloth from Spain, linens from Egypt, and homespuns from nearby in Italy also came to the shops of the Roman tailors to be fashioned into the simply-made garments in common use. The extent to which raw materials were shipped to Rome to be woven into cloth, on the other hand, must be determined on the basis of very slim evidence.

Household Production. For the wealthy private households the problem is simple: from the inscriptions in the great columbaria of the first century it is clear that spinning maids, weavers, and the supervising *lanipendiae* were occupied with the preparation of cloth which private tailors (*vestiarii*) made into garments.[34] The slaves in Lepidus' household were spinning at the looms when the mob broke into the atrium (Ascon., *in Milo.*, p. 38 [Stangl]); Augustus prided himself on wearing homemade garments (Suet., *Aug.*, 73); and the *mulieres lanifices* with their equipment appear in the legacies discussed by the early jurists.[35] Such establishments, however, belonged only to the wealthy; even a comparatively well-to-do magis-

---

[34] In the vault of the Statilii Tauri, for example, we find eight spinners, one supervisor of the wool, four patchers, four weavers, two dyers, four fullers, and one shoemaker (*C. I. L.*, VI, 6213-6640; the vault was in use for about five generations, Westermann, " Sklaverei," *P.-W.*, Suppl. VI, 1038). In the household of Livia Augusta (VI 3926-4326) were two fullers, five patchers, two supervisors, six women in charge of clothing (*a veste*), two dyers, one maker of cloaks (*paenularius*), one tailor, and one shoemaker. These two groups are the largest known: there are 370 *loculi* in the vault of Taurus and about 600 in that of Livia.

[35] Ser. Sulpicius Rufus, *Dig.*, 33, 7, 16, 2; Trebatius, *ibid.*, 12, 5.

trate like Cicero found it necessary to hire special weavers.[36] Though the main purpose of such domestic production was undoubtedly to supply the needs of the household, it is not necessary to assume that it was the sole objective: Atticus, it will be remembered, made clothing for Cicero on his estate at Epirus, and there is some proof that a few men like him and Crassus transformed their *familiae* into efficient business units.[37]

The needs of but a small part of the million inhabitants of the capital would be met by industry of this nature. Nor is it very likely that the wives of petty shopkeepers spent their time, when they were not assisting their husbands, in preparing cloth for the family's use; records of retail clothing dealers are too numerous at Rome for such a supposition. Yet we look in vain for inscriptions of professional weavers [38] or for records of weavers' guilds, as in Etruria. If a domestic system took the place of the guilds in this industry there would be no supporting evidence; for either the entrepreneur would be known by another title such as "fullo"[39] or he would be an Atticus or a Crassus, who owned a large body of household slaves and freedmen. From Juvenal comes the one

---

[36] Special carpenters as well as weavers were hired for specified periods (Park, *The Plebs in Cicero's Day*, diss. Bryn Mawr, 1921, 61).

[37] Atticus, of course ran a publishing business, but factors at work here would be applicable to other industrial enterprises. In Nepos' biography (13, 3) it is stated that in addition to slaves catering to domestic needs there were young slaves trained as readers, many copyists, and *not even a footman who could not perform both of these offices well*. There are several interesting implications in these lines. In the first place, unlike modern business men, Atticus had no office but made use of his household and the slaves attached to it. For the same reason the strong box of the Pompeian auctioneer, Caecilius Jucundus, was found in the *tablinum* of his home. In the second place, when Atticus' publishing business demanded, all the slaves— doorkeepers, footmen, weavers—were pressed into service. We shall hear later of other business men who probably used their *familia* in the same way: Fannius, Remmius Palaemon, and Crassus. It would be unwarranted, however, to believe that wealthy aristocrats like Statilius Taurus, the Volusii, or Junius Silanus (all of whose columbaria have been excavated and whose personal retinue is known) were interested in the profits from trade. Households like that of Atticus would probably be rare.

[38] The *lintearii* of the inscriptions (VI, 7468 and 9526) were both late (3rd or 4th century).

[39] See Frank, *An Economic History*, 261-3.

piece of evidence for a group of skilled weavers outside the household, and the interpretation of this passage is at best unreliable.[40]

Fulling. For Pompeii there are rather suggestive indications that the fullers had performed the function of the clothier, organizing the varied steps in the woolen industry.[41] At Rome the great fullers' guild (the *conlegium aquae, C. I. L.,* VI, 10298) had been in existence before the time of Augustus, and the rules of the group (the *lex conlegii*) have been preserved, if only in a fragmentary state. Unfortunately, though they throw some light on the activities of the members, the regulations are concerned chiefly with concessions granted them by the state. With most of those involving the duties of the guild officers we have no concern, but in line 14 begin the following significant conditions: *Pro conlegio ni quis fulloniam fecisse nive cretulentum exigisse velit nisi in duabus lacunis populi Romani jus emet. Qui contra fecerit adversus eum qui volet rem conlegii gerere liceto.* In other words, to belong to the guild a fuller had to pay a tax to the state for the use of two *lacus* (probably public fountains).[42] It seems, then, that this important group of urban fullers was concerned chiefly with cleaning *ab usu* or possibly with the finishing of cloth that had just left the loom; there is certainly no evidence that they were engaged in the distribution of the finished product.

To the authorized members of this guild the state had early granted special privileges in regard to the use of water from the public aqueducts (Frontinus, *De Aquaeductu Urbis Ro-*

---

[40] Juv., 8, 42-3 : Ut te conciperet quae sanguine fulget Iuli
        Non quae ventoso conducta sub aggere texit.
Friedländer (*ad loc.*) declares that the "conducta" was either a poor woman at work in her small apartment or in a large weaving factory.

[41] The cloth-hall built by Eumachia in the Forum for the use of the fullers seems to indicate that these men not only finished the cloth but also distributed it (Frank, *ibid.*). The building is discussed by Mau, *Pompeii,* 107-114, especially 108.

[42] This explanation of Mommsen, published in the Corpus, has been accepted in all subsequent discussions. See also the commentary in Bruns, *Fontes Juris Romani Antiqui,* 1909, 394-6. The inscription was found on the Esquiline near the spot made famous by the litigations of the third century (VI, 266).

mae, 94 and 98). Other concessions are revealed by the famous twenty-year lawsuit of the third century (VI, 266) which resulted in a complete victory of the fullers over the *curator aquarum.*[43] When this officer of the government had demanded that the members pay rent for a *locus publicus* (probably the ground surrounding a public fountain) the officials of the guild were able to prove *ex eo tempore ex quo Augustus rempublicam obtinere coepit usque in hodier(num) numquam haec loca pensiones pensitasse.* The exemption from tax in all likelihood included the amount usually paid for obtaining water from public aqueducts. The scene named in the dispute was the Esquiline near such an aqueduct, and at the time of the decision of the first jurist, Aelius Florianus, the property was already decorated with sacred statues. It is not unreasonable to suppose that there was also a building where this organized guild held its meetings. Government concessions and the pleasures of sociability probably brought most of the smaller independent fullers at Rome into the fold.

From the regulations governing membership in the guild of fullers, it would seem that the ordinary establishments were of considerable size. Even if the greater part of the activity of these independent workmen was concerned with finishing homespuns and cleaning soiled garments, these functions alone required expensive equipment and skilled workmen.[44] At Pompeii, too, such requirements had removed fulling from the confines of the single small shop;[45] and private fulleries were, of course, impossible except in the most wealthy households.[46] Information about the social and economic status of these men, however, is almost entirely lacking, for in addition to the inscriptions of the great guild, there are only two which mention fullers not in an organized *collegium* (VI 9429-30: freedmen with Greek cognomina).[47]

---

[43] Discussed by Waltzing, II, 472-3; by Pernier, "Fullones," *D. E.,* III, 321; by Jacob, "Fullonica," *D.-S.,* 1351.

[44] For the details see Blümner, 170-183 and Pernier, 316-17.

[45] See Mau, *Pompeii,* 412-416.

[46] The household of Statilius Taurus (VI, 6287-90), of Livia (3970), of Marcellus (4445), of Drusus (4336), etc.

[47] A *collegium,* which was probably no more than a number of

At Pompeii the accounts of Caecilius Jucundus show that this famous capitalist had rented from the municipality fulleries over which he had set his slaves or freedmen as agents.[48] To these workrooms came quantities of homespuns from neighboring villas. At Rome, too, there were probably investments of like nature, for there is an inscription of an unknown freedman (he is designated by the initials M. P. R.) who directed the *Fullonicae Philipporum* of Marcus Philippus in much the same way as Primus had managed the workshops of Jucundus.[49]

It is safe to conclude that most of the clothing for the poorer working class was imported from Italian and Gallic mills; so the discussion of numerous inscriptions of the *sagarii,* dealers in such wares, belong more properly under distribution. The *vestiarii,* too, although they undoubtedly fitted togas and sewed together the two pieces of cloth that formed the tunic, were busy with the ready-to-wear trade.[50] Some attention, however, must be paid to the spinning and weaving that went on in large households, for in this industry it is likely that domestic production supplied not only the needs of the families of the rich but to a small extent those of an outside market. Whether the urban fuller had any rôle in this system must still remain doubtful; there are no clear indications from the inscriptions that their activities extended beyond cleaning and fulling to distribution.

The Centonarii. In the case of the *centonarii,* however, there is evidence of production and even of distribution on an

---

workmen running a fullery, is known from an inscription of the early second century (VI, 404: *collegium sanctissimum quod consistit in praedis Larci Macedonis*). It is not necessary to conclude that the consular Macedo had any interest in the profits or the activities of these fullers; the group merely had its workrooms on his estate. This interpretation is strengthened by the fact that T. Flavius Successus, who dedicated the honorary inscription and was probably a leading member of the group, was an imperial freedman. Successus may well have been the entrepreneur who had organized and financed the enterprise.

[48] The wax tablets recording the payment of the rent are published in Part I of the Supplement to *C. I. L.,* IV, no. 141.

[49] Pernier, 320.

[50] Ulpian (*Dig.,* 14, 3, 5, 4) contrasts the *vestiarius* with the weaver (*lintearius*). See also Chapot, "Vestiarius," *D.-S.,* 760-1.

unusual scale. From patches cut from worn garments these workmen made wrappers for slaves to wear over their new tunics, cheap blankets for the poor, saddle cloths, and even coverings for implements of warfare.[51] In most of the cities of the empire the guild formed by the union of *centonarii* and *fabri* served as the local fire department, for the woolen blankets of the ragmen and the axes and ladders of the carpenters were invaluable instruments in checking the spread of the flames. Since at Rome, on the other hand, the *vigiles* established by the government performed this civic function, the *centonarii* were apparently only makers or dealers in *centones*.[52]

Nevertheless, all of the makers of patch-work garments known from inscriptions at Rome were members of a guild which continued in existence from the late republic (in the time of Augustus it was celebrating its fifty-fifth anniversary: VI, 7861) until the fourth century. Four of the inscriptions relating to the *collegium* were found in the columbarium of the Octavii, and with one exception (VI, 7862, L. Tuccius Mario) the chief guild officers were freedmen of a Lucius Octavius. They include Secundus, the president, his two brothers who served as messengers and sergeants-at-arms (*viatores*), and Cerdo and Diomedes, members of the " senate." At first glance these circumstances suggest a domestic guild formed by the workmen in the *familia* of a rich Octavius; they may just as well, however, indicate that members of the household were important members of the organized *centonarii* of the city, who before obtaining their freedom had worked as slaves in the shops of their patron.[53] Since the names of only the highest guild officials have been recorded, other Lucii Octavii may also have had their names on the

---

[51] See Kubitschek, " Cento," *P.-W.*, III, 1932-3.

[52] This conclusion is strengthened by the fact that the Roman *dendrophoroi* (who were often associated in the fire brigades with the *fabri* and *centonarii*) apparently have no civic function but were organized into a religious guild (VI, 641-2, 1925, 30973). For these guilds in provincial cities see Gatti, " Centonarius," *D. E.*, II[1], 180-2.

[53] Waltzing, I, 282, n. 5. See also II, 112, where all the inscriptions are dated in approximately the same period of the first century.

club's album. If these suppositions are valid, the original workroom of Lucius was of considerable size.[54] Material success among the laborers who stitched together patches or the small dealers who distributed the finished blankets would be rare. Consequently, L. Sextilius Seleucus, a decurion of the guild who made a donation of 10,000 denarii ($2,000) to his fellow members (VI, 9254), was in all probability the owner of a chain of shops or of a workroom of considerable size. In view of the fact that the interest on the amount (about $120) was to be used for a banquet to celebrate the birthday of Augustus, the guild may well have consisted of several hundred members,[55] many of whom undoubtedly worked for Seleucus. Thus all the inscriptional evidence relating to the activity of these makers of patchwork garments argues against the small-shop system. Furthermore, the necessity of collecting cast-off clothing in considerable quantities favored the concentration of many stitchers in one workroom.

Dyeing. With the *purpurarii* as with the *centonarii* and *vestiarii* there is the same familiar union of artisan and merchant: one dyer definitely calls himself an *infector* (VI, 33861, C. Lutius Abdeus); some twenty others are merely " dealers in purple." Although the city was not a centre for the preparation of this dye and Eastern vessels were constantly importing the best Tyrian purple cloth,[56] it was the Roman

---

[54] The location of only one shop belonging to a *centonarius* is known, in the Subura by the *Turris Mamilia* (VI, 33837). Since the inscription giving this information has been found near the funeral monument of the Octavii (see *B. C.*, XVI [1888], 398), it is likely that the two freedmen (M. Octavius M. l. Marcio and M. Octavius M. l. Attalus) who ran the shop were working as *institores* for the account of their former master. Moreover, as Marcio continued the tradition of an Octavius as president of the ragmen's guild, his patron may also have continued the traditional investment of the family in the large-scale production of *centones*.

[55] The makers of citrus wood tables inlaid with ivory who formed a guild at Rome in Hadrian's day (VI, 33885) were each given 5 denarii ($1) as a *sportula* on the emperor's birthday and 3 on the birthday of their patron. The donation was an important item in the expense account of the banquet.

[56] Hammer-Jensen, " Färbung," *P.-W.*, Suppl. III, 462. Even when the manufacture of purple cloth became a state monopoly, the city was not one of the nine places in the west having a *procurator baphiorum*.

negotiatores found guilty of selling *pauculas uncias* whose shops were closed by Nero's edict against the use of amethystine and Tyrian colors (Suet., *Nero, 32*). Pliny's "consumers' research" also implies that purchasers were interested in the price of the dye (9, 137).[57] Consequently, it is not improbable that some of the urban *purpurarii* were dealers in coloring matter. Nevertheless, the great need for dyers at Rome in redyeing faded clothing as well as in the preparation of new cloth, joined with the almost complete absence of inscriptions of *tinctores* and *infectores* (so numerous at Pompeii), forces us to consider the possibility that the dyers have chosen the more elegant term *purpurarius* to cover their manifold activities. Their title, adopted from this most popular and lasting color, gives no indication of the rich vermilions, azures, and saffrons at their disposal.

Among the Roman dyers known from the inscriptions are numerous freedmen and freedwomen of the *gens Veturia*. The shop of D. Veturius D. l. Atticus and his wife, Veturia Tryphera, was on the Vicus Jugarius (*N. S.,* 1922, 144); L. Plutius L. l. Eros, his wife, Veturia C. C. l. Attica, and a freedwoman, Auge, operated a shop on the more fashionable Vicus Tuscus (XIV, 2433). Again, among the freedmen of D. Veturius D. l. Diogenes (VI, 37820) is listed a freedwoman engaged in work with purple, whose shop was in the northern section of the Esquiline near the Monumenta Mariana.[58] The woman is the only member of the group whose occupation is named, but it is probable that her patron (himself a freedman of D. Veturius) was also interested in the dyeing industry. Considering the chance nature of inscriptional evidence, the survival of so many *purpurarii* who had formerly been slaves of a Decimus Veturius offers several possibilities. Veturius may have operated a large dyeing establishment where his former slaves had learned their trade, and

---

[57] Pliny (*ibid.*) quotes Nepos as saying that violet dye cost 100 denarii a pound in his youth (80-70 B. C.) and that Tyrian dye, first used in 63 B. C., cost 1,000 denarii.

[58] Gatti (*B. C.,* XXXV [1907], 355-6) has identified the location. See also the large group of freedwomen of A. Vicirius who were *purpurariae* (VI, 9846).

they, after manumission, may have established the independent shops enumerated above. On the other hand, these freedmen may have been foremen of branch shops under Veturius' control, possibly working on a commission basis; for like the wealthy Umbricius Scaurus at Pompeii, Veturius may have found it less profitable to keep the entire firm under one roof.[59]

The preceding group of inscriptions has been singled out for special consideration because of its uniqueness. The dozen or so others picture a more representative system of work: the small artisan sales booth run by a proprietor with one or two freedmen.[60]

Shoemaking. Because of the need of workrooms of considerable size and of elaborate and expensive equipment, tanning was naturally conducted on a large scale.[61] The inscriptions, however, record nothing but the names of a few tanners: two *coriarii* from Christian times (*C. I. L.*, VI, 9280-1), an importer who supplied the city's tanneries with skins (9667: P. Juventius Successus, *negotias coriariorum*),[62] and a slave helper who prepared the hides before they were sent to the tannery (9279: Cleomenes, *coriarius subactarius*).

The only reference to a guild of these workmen at Rome occurs in the fourth century (1682: about 334 A. D.) when the *corpus* was in the service of the state. Its earlier existence, however, is implied in this decree thanking the prefect of the city, its present patron, for restoring the workrooms (*insulae*) in accordance with imperial rescripts dating from the end of the second century.[63] These tanners' workshops, in the special district across the Tiber to which they had been relegated, had undoubtedly existed from the first century (Pl., 17, 51; Mart., 6, 93, 1-4; Juv., 14, 203). A more exact location is

---

[59] Frank (*Econ. Hist.*, 259) bases this conclusion on the names of the varied brands: *gari flos ex officina Scauri, ab Umbricia*, etc.

[60] For example, *C. I. L.*, VI, 9843-48, 33861, etc.

[61] Mau, "Coriarius," *P.-W.*, IV, 1227-31; Blümner, 271-3.

[62] L. Nerusius Mithres, who imported goat skins from the Sabine territory to Rome, is known from *C. I. L.*, IX, 4796.

[63] The implication is that the workrooms and sales booths were rented from the state, perhaps in some public basilica (see Waltzing, II, 521).

given by the Regionary Catalogue (for region XIV), according to which the *Coriaria Septimiana* extended along the river
bank between the temple of Fors Fortuna and the Porta
Septimiana. In 1889-90, moreover, the remains of a tannery
were discovered in this district: beneath the church of S.
Cecilia there were six vats (1.3 m. in diameter and 1.4 deep)
resembling those familiar from tanning establishments at
Pompeii.[64] Though the date of the establishment is unknown,
the excellent brick work precludes a very late period. It is
not improbable that the vats were part of the workroom of an
independent tanner who belonged to the guild in its earlier
years.

Having secured their leather from the tanners, the cob-
blers repaired to the small booth which served them both as
workshop and salesroom. Although there was possibly some
concentration in the Argiletum [65] and the Vicus Sandaliarius,[66] shoemakers' shops are known from all sections of the
city: *post Castores* (Pl., 10, 122), *de Subura* (*C. I. L.,* VI,
9284), *a Porta Fontinale* (VI, 7544), *a Spem Vetere* (XV,
5929), and *ab luco Semeles* (VI, 9897). The shop sign of a
sutor a Porta Fontinale, an imperial freedman of the age of
the Flavians, shows specialization in the making of the heavy
nailed boot known as the *caligula.*[67] Records of such *caligarii*
(see also VI, 9225) and other specialists like *crepidarii*
(makers of slippers: 9284 and 7544), and a *solatarius* (maker
of women's shoes: 9897) in all likelihood indicate rather
large establishments where good shoes were made to measure.

Proof of the great number of shoemakers at work in the city
is given by the inscription of the *collegium perpetuum fabrum*

---

[64] See Hülsen, " Coriaria Septimiana," *P.-W.,* IV, 1227 and Platner-
Ashby, *ad loc.*

[65] The place named by Martial (2, 17, 1-3) may apply to the upper
end of the Argiletum where it meets the Subura, and so equally well
to the Vicus Sandaliarius.

[66] The Atrium Sutorium was probably located here during the first
century (Varro, *Ling. Lat.,* 6, 14; Festus, p. 480 [Lindsay]; *C. I. L.,*
I, p. 315). This building may have served as a sales and display
centre as well as a collective series of workrooms.

[67] See *B. C.,* XV (1887), 52-56. Helvius' business was obviously
more successful than that of the ordinary cobbler, for in addition to
the imposing sign, he had a freedman helper.

soliarium baxiarium (VI, 9404), makers of women's light slippers from papyrus or plant fabric. This guild had three " centuries " of members: in other words, there were three hundred shoemakers producing a special type of women's shoes in Rome at one time.

The other organized group of shoe dealers, a guild of wholesale dealers in soles (VI, 1117 and 1118, *corpus coriariorum magnariorum et solatariorum*), whose meeting place was in the trans-Tiberine district near the tanners' vats, can be definitely dated in the late third century.[68] It is quite possible that the phrase, *immunis Romae regionibus XIIII,* applied to the president of the women's slipper makers' guild, indicates the late date of that organization also.

V. THE BUILDING TRADE

The Contract System. The system of letting out the erection of state buildings to independent contractors in use during the late republic is revealed very clearly in Cicero's account of Verres' misuse of funds in the repair of the Temple of Castor.[69] Further evidence of the method is furnished by the inscription describing the repaving of the Via Caecilia.[70] The precaution taken by the administration at this time against careless work is shown by the inscriptions from the Pons Fabricius: the contract for making the wooden bridge into a stone one was let in 62 B. C., but it was not until 40 years later that the consuls of the year 21 declared that the work had been duly and satisfactorily completed.[71]

It is often assumed, however, that in the empire the work on public buildings was placed more and more in the hands of

---

[68] See Waltzing, II, 370 and IV, 13. The *solatarii* were wholesale dealers in soles or in skins prepared by the tanners (Lafaye, " Coriarius," *D.-S.,* 1507).

[69] Cicero, *In Verrem,* 2, 130 ff. In 144 it is stated that the job was let for 560,000 sesterces ($28,000), the contractors furnishing the materials and their own or hired workmen. Details of the contract are contained in sec. 143 ff.

[70] *C. I. L.,* I², 808 (time of Sulla). These contracts were let to freedmen, not to knights. The cost for paving was approximately 1 to 2.2 asses (about 1.75 to 3 cents) the sq. ft. (*Econ. Surv.,* I, 373).

[71] *C. I. L.,* I, 600 and VI, 1305; also Lanciani, *Ruins and Excavations,* 17-18.

imperial freedmen and gangs of imperial slaves. Support adduced for this assumption is of several kinds. In the first place, there have been found in the burial vaults of the imperial house numerous slaves of freedmen designated as *architecti, fabri, mensores, marmorarii,* etc.[72] Furthermore, a model for slave labor of this type is furnished by the gang of 240 slaves organized by Agrippa and bequeathed to Augustus (to be supplemented by 460 imperial slaves under Claudius) for guarding, repairing, and building the aqueducts.[73] Those who assume the existence of similar groups for other building projects fail to distinguish between the permanent need for workers on the aqueducts—a need which made a trained corps a constant necessity—and the sporadic demand for labor on ordinary building projects. Too much importance, moreover, must not be given to the group of slaves, trained as builders and organized on the model of the army into legions and cohorts, which accompanied the Emperor Hadrian on his tour of the provinces.[74] Time and the possible scarcity of skilled labor were factors which might operate in distant localities but not at Rome.

Guilds of Builders. Though there can be no doubt that imperial slaves were constantly employed in state projects at Rome, some stress must be laid on the complexity of the situation and on the existence of other types of workingmen who continued to make their livelihood as builders in the capital. The importance of the carpenters' guild (*collegium fabrum tignuariorum*) is attested by unusually full epigraphi-

---

[72] *Marmorarii* (VI, 8893, 9102), a *marmoribus* (410, 8482-6); *lapidarii* (8871), *fabri* (3969, 4443, 4446, 9102), *architecti* (5738, 8724-26, etc.), *pictores* (4008, 9102), *tectores,* etc. See also Westermann, "Sklaverei," *P.-W.,* Suppl. VI, 1035-6; Gummerus, "Industrie," *P.-W.,* IX, 1461.

[73] Frontinus, 98 and 116. The cost of the Claudian aqueduct ($17,500,000), however, is much too great for the materials and the hauling. During the republic this work had been let to private contractors by the ediles. The contractor furnished his own slaves, but they were under official supervision (Westermann, 1036). In the time of Augustus the slaves of the state were under the control of senatorial *curatores aquarum;* in that of Claudius, under imperial freedmen, *procuratores aquarum.*

[74] Aurelius Victor, *Epit.,* 14, 5 (see Waltzing, II, 121-2).

cal evidence.[75] In this guild during the years 198-210 A. D. there were 60 *decuriones*, 60 officers in charge of groups composed of at least 10 members (VI, 1060). It would be unwise, however, to place the number of members at 600, for inscriptions of the same group from an earlier period prove that the decuries included over 20 members, and at times probably more.[76] The guild, then, in the late second century may have been composed of 1,000 to 1,500 members, too large a number of builders to be relegated to small, extra-official jobs. It is clear, moreover, that the guild was in existence in the late republican period and continued to function until the fourth century (*Cod. Theod.*, 12, 1, 62), though its size during these centuries may have varied. Since the inscriptions give only the names of the members, it is difficult to determine their exact status. None were slaves; some were undoubtedly freedmen; and others were expressly designated as freeborn.[77] In view of these facts, it is not likely that the thousand or more guild members were unskilled laborers; rather they were successful carpenters who could control the services of numerous slaves. To suggest that there were many like Crassus in the group is, of course, unwise, but his practice of renting out or employing slave gangs of considerable size undoubtedly continued.[78] Perhaps an analogy may be drawn

---

[75] According to Asconius (p. 59 [Stangl]) this had been one of the guilds recognized by the senate as serving public needs, and according to the inscriptions the date of its official reorganization fell in 7 B. C. (VI, 10299). Inscriptions of the guild in chronological order are as follows: VI, 30982 (2 B. C.-3 A. D.); 9034 (79-83 A. D.); 996 (104-108); 321 (109-113); 148 (124-128; cf. also 9406); 10299 (124-138); 1060 (198-218); 9415b (204-9). See also Gummerus, "Darstellungen aus dem Handwerk auf römischen Grab- und Votivsteinen," *Jahrbuch des kaiserlich deutschen archäologischen Instituts*, XXVIII (1913), 91, and Liebenam, *D. E.*, III, 8-18.

[76] One of the presidents of the guild gave to the 10th decury a burial place with 33 niches (VI, 9405). At the time of the donation, however, the decury had 22 members.

[77] Among the 54 names in VI, 1060 filiation occurs only twice. Freeborn members, however, are found in VI, 996 (31220a) and 9405. Since there is such a preponderance of Latin cognomina over Greek among the members, Gummerus has suggested (*P.-W.*, 1503) that these *fabri* were foremen and contractors for building projects.

[78] Plutarch, *Crassus*, 2: "And besides this, observing how natural and familiar at Rome were such fatalities as the conflagration and

6

between members of the Roman guild and the *fabri* at Ostia. Here, where more information is available about their wealth and social position, were carpenters who became *Augustales,* knights, and even town magistrates.[79]

None of the other guilds connected with the building industry at the capital reached such size or prominence, but the existence of varied types of organized groups is noteworthy. Under Titus a guild known as the *collegium subrutor(um)* (*C. I. L.,* VI, 940) was engaged in tearing down dilapidated buildings or those harmed by fire. The *collegium subaedianorum* (VI, 9558-9 = 33875-6) was probably composed of carpenters who worked on panels, cornices, and balustrades for the interiors of houses and public buildings.[80] The *conlegium secto(rum) serrarium* (VI, 9888), in existence from the time of the republic, was undoubtedly formed by stonecutters. Among the organized *marmorarii* were stone dressers, cutters of inscriptions, and even sculptors (VI, 9550).[81] Finally, a *collegium pavimentariorum,* a guild of pavers, is recorded for the year 19 A. D. (VI, 243). This group like the *mensores aedificiorum* and the *collegium structorum* (VI,

---

collapse of buildings, . . . he proceeded to buy slaves who were architects and builders. Then, when he had *over 500* of these, he would constantly buy houses that caught fire and houses adjoining these, for these their owners would let go at a trifling price, owing to their fear and uncertainty. . . . But though he owned so many artisans, he built no house for himself other than the one in which he lived." The passage has been discussed by Gummerus, "Die Bauspekulation des Crassus," *Klio,* XVI (1920), 190-2. Gummerus' conclusion is that Crassus did not rent out his gang to building contractors, but employed them in rebuilding the demolished houses so he could resell them at higher prices.

[79] See Frank, "The People of Ostia," *Cl. J.,* XXIX (1934), 484-6.

[80] So Lafaye, "Marmorarius," *D.-S.,* 1605-6; Waltzing, II, 122. The *marmorarius subaedanus* (VI, 33293) may have prepared the marble veneer and the columns used for similar purposes.

[81] A drawing of the workshop of a *marmorarius* from a tombstone now lost (VI, 19312) has been preserved (Gummerus, "Darstellungen," 95). A man in a toga, probably the owner, is pictured with a roll in his hand; another man is hewing through a stone block with a large saw. Two other workmen are cutting stone blocks: one using a hammer and chisel, the other a plumbline. It is not improbable that other members of the guild had workrooms of comparable size. Independent *marmorarii* are named in the following inscriptions: VI, 37577, 9552-6, 16534, 33930, 9102, and 9551.

444) may have been composed of imperial slaves, though the evidence is indecisive.[82]

The relationship of guilds of free laborers to the building commissioners appointed by the emperors or to his architects and procurators cannot be defined with any certainty,[83] but a valuable inscription from the time of Domitian (VI, 9034) throws some light on the problem. An imperial freedman, Ti. Claudius Aug. l. Onesimus, who is a *redemptor operum Caesaris* (a contractor employed on state jobs), has become the chief magistrate in the carpenters' guild. Evidently Onesimus' former services as slave in the imperial household had helped him to secure such contracts, and this privileged position had forced his colleagues to recognize him as a valuable member of their organization. It is interesting, moreover, to see that the contract system was being used for state enterprises about 80 A. D., a situation to which other inscriptions of *redemptores* bear testimony.[84] The buildings which the emperors undertook in Italy were frequently let out to contractors: *redemptor operum Caesarum* (IX, 4694) and *redemptor operum Caesarum et puplicorum (sic)* (XIV, 3530; see also XIV, 2091).

One of the methods used for imperial projects, then, involved the following steps. First, an architect was selected by the emperor to plan the proposed structure. Though the

---

[82] The *mensores aedificiorum* are discussed by Hirschfeld, *Verwaltungs.*, 256 and by Fabricius, "Mensor," *P.-W.*, XV[1], 959-60.

[83] For the officials in charge of building projects during the empire see Hirschfeld, 265-72. In the early period commissions were only infrequently entrusted to imperial slaves and freedmen: it was not until Trajan's time that an imperial freedman was the administrator of the *opera publica* (VI, 8479 and XI, 3860). From the time of Claudius, however, the imperial slaves known as *mensores* had been paid directly from the fiscus and were not under the supervision of the *curatores operum publicorum* (VI, 8933). These surveyors were probably used to check the efficiency of work done by independent contractors.

[84] A contractor for interior carpentry is recorded in *N. S.*, 1924, 348, though it should be noted that he was a former slave in the imperial household. A *redemptor mar(morum?)* (a contractor to supply marble or work in marble) is known from VI, 33873, and a *redemptor* who supplied sand for various building projects is named in XV, 7150. The work of the *redemptor a laco Fundan(o)* (VI, 9854) cannot be defined. Contractors for the repair of streets in the empire are mentioned in VI, 8468-9 and 31338.

Roman feeling that the credit for public buildings belonged to the state prevented the inscribing of architects' names on imperial structures, the most famous have been preserved in the sources: Rabirius, whose originality found expression in the imposing scale and the innovations of the Colosseum and the Thermae Titi; [85] Apollodorus, who designed the Forum of Trajan, Trajan's famous bridge across the Danube, and the Pantheon; [86] Severus and Celer, who were probably responsible for the development of the brick-faced concrete construction which came to the fore in the Age of Nero (Tac., *Ann.*, 15, 42); Vitruvius and the architects and military engineers named in the preface to his first book; [87] and the Emperor Hadrian himself.[88] Some of these men were undoubtedly Greek *peregrini* like the famous Apollodorus of Damascus; others were probably Roman military engineers who were placed in charge of civil jobs.[89] Their plans were let by imperial freedmen or senatorial commissions to contractors, and they, in turn, employed the *fabri tignuarii* and *marmorarii* mentioned above.

The common labor used in building operations at Rome must have been varied: imperial slaves,[90] slave gangs of pri-

[85] Rabirius is mentioned by Martial in 7, 56, where he is praised as the designer of Domitian's palace on the Palatine. See Rivoira, *Roman Architecture* (trans. by Rushforth), 1925, 84.
[86] For his work under Trajan see Dio, 69, 4 and Procopius, *de Aedif.*, 4, 6, 6. According to Dio (*ibid.*) Hadrian sent to Apollodorus his own designs for the temple of Venus and Roma to show that important buildings could be erected at the capital without his help.
[87] M. Aurelius, P. Minidius, and Cn. Cornelius.
[88] For Hadrian as an architect see Rivoira, 83.
[89] See Duff, *Freedmen in the Early Roman Empire*, 1928, 122-3. Inscriptions of architects are relatively scarce, but of the five independent architects in the sixth volume of the *Corpus* (8725 and 9151-4) three, at least, are freedmen of Oriental or Greek extraction. An architect from Bithynia is also recorded on an inscription in *N. S.*, 1924, 425. It should be noted, too, that when Pliny asked Trajan to send him an architect to Bithynia, Trajan replied that he lived in the midst of them (Pl., *Ep.*, 10, 39 and 40). Duff concludes that native-born Romans held aloof from this profession, and that Roman names like Celer or Rabirius probably mean only that a freedman had adopted a more honorary title. See, however, Rivoira (85-8), who insists that the Italian-born mechanical engineers were the architects responsible for the new developments in concrete construction.
[90] Although it is often difficult to distinguish between *servi Cae-*

vate entrepreneurs,[91] state prisoners,[92] soldiers,[93] and even the free *plebs urbana*. This latter group is mentioned in an anecdote from Suetonius' life of Vespasian (18). When an engineer who had invented a machine for hoisting large columns, in the expectation of a great reward, presented his scheme to the emperor, he was dismissed with these words: " How could I then take care of my poor? " The story, however, gains in point if placed in its historical setting. Vespasian came to the throne as the first representative of a new dynasty which had to make some bid for popular favor. In addition, he found a city wrecked by Nero's fire and the devastation of the year of the four emperors. These conditions made building on a large scale a necessity and offered the new ruler an opportunity to appeal to the unemployed. The Colosseum, the restoration of the Capitoline Temple and the Claudian aqueduct, and the removal of the Golden House for the erection of buildings for public uses were the results. It might even be possible to find in the tremendous building projects of later emperors a similar attempt to substitute state labor for doles and thus to secure their position on the throne.

Private Building. Private building activities seem of small moment in comparison with imperial projects; but the number of homes built at Rome during the early empire was certainly very great, and there can be no question of their magnifi-

---

saris and *servi publici*, the emperor was probably the largest slave-owner in the Roman world (Westermann, 1035 and Gummerus, *P.-W.*, 1458).

[91] Vitruvius (7, 1, 3) speaks of *decuriae* of *tectores* who were called in to ram down the rubble for pavements. Large groups would certainly be available in the city: Crassus, it will be remembered, had 500; M. Egnatius Rufus, edile in 21 B. C., could form a fire brigade for Rome from his own and a few hired slaves (Dio, 53, 24); Pedanius Secundus, *praefectus urbis* in 61 A. D., had 400 slaves at hand (Tac., *Ann.*, 14, 43, 4); etc.

[92] Suet., *Nero*, 31: " For the execution of these projects (the Golden House, the canal from Avernus to Ostia) he had given orders that the prisoners all over the empire should be transported to Italy," etc.

[93] See Cozzo, *Ingegneria Romana*, 70. Here is discussed an inscription (*N. S.*, 1915, 137-41) in which 98 members of the *decuria Quinti Arrunti Surai* are detailed to complete 4214 ft. of earthwork fortification: i. e., 43 ft. per man. The employment of soldiers in building streets, roads, etc., is treated in the same place.

cence.[94] Details about this branch of the industry come chiefly
from Cicero's letters at the end of the republic and from the
rare representations on tombstones which show the departed
at his earthly pursuits.[95] As in the case of public buildings
the plans for Tullia's shrine were drawn by the freeborn architect Cluatius (ad Att., 12, 18, 45), but since the work was
not completed, the system of letting the construction contract
is unknown. For the Manilian villa, however, the architect
Caesius also served as redemptor, acting as a go-between for
his master and the builder Diphilus (ad Quint. Frat., 3, 1, 2).
In the rebuilding of a city residence for Quintus Cicero the
slave vilicus Nicephor had accepted the contract for the
whole job at a total cost of 16,000 sest. ($800; ibid., 5).[96]
The types of workmen available for special parts of the job
are indicated to some extent by specialists named on the inscriptions: marmorarii (VI, 9556, 9462, 9551, etc.), fabri
intestinarii (VI, 9401, 9415[a], etc.), structor parietarius (VI,
9910), fabri subaediani (VI, 9558-9), and structores (VI,
9909).

VI. METAL WORK

Gold. Of all the industrial activities of the city we are
best informed about the work in precious metals, for it is
clear that during the first century of the empire Rome became an important centre for the making of jewelry and
precious plate.[97] From the capital come 138 of the 187 Ital-

---

[94] Pliny (36, 109) says that the house of Lepidus, the finest in the
city when Catulus was consul, within 35 years was not the hun-
dredth in rank. Seneca (Ep., 90, 9-10) mentions the long drays
laden with fir and pine for the coffered ceilings of private homes.
[95] Collected by Gummerus, "Darstellungen," 85-118. One of the
most interesting is the relief from the grave of the Hateri (see VI,
19148-51), which shows the crane, the pulleys, and treadmills used
by these large building contractors.
[96] In another instance Cicero paid the contractor half the sum
stipulated when the work had progressed to an agreed stage (ad
Quint. Frat., 2, 4, 3). See also 2, 5, 3, where a redemptor is carrying out the plan of the architect multis structoribus.
[97] This is the conclusion of Gummerus in "Die römische Industrie," Klio, XV-XVI (1918-20), 256-302 at 262. The distribution of
inscriptions is as follows: 21 from the provinces, 28 from other cities
of Italy, 80 from Rome (independent artisans), 25 mentioning slave
or freedmen artisans in private households at Rome, and 33 naming
officials of the imperial palace engaged in the care of jewelry and
silver plate.

ian inscriptions mentioning artisans engaged in this work, and goldsmiths or engravers migrating to other cities speak with pride of their activity at the capital.[98] Three conditions fostered this blossoming: an abundant supply of raw materials, the demands of a rich population, and the presence of a great number of skilled artists from the Hellenized East. The large amount of gold from state-owned mines and of gems from Africa and India directed to the city has already been discussed; further, proof of the intricacy of the city's demands is offered not only by Pliny's tirades against the lavish use of jewelry (33, 40-1) but by the appearance of such specialized titles among workers in gold as *aurifices, brattiarii, inauratores, auri nextrices,* and *barbaricarii*; finally, the numbers of trained workmen who, at the end of the republic, came into the households of the emperors and rich senators as slaves may be inferred from the numerous inscriptions recording the freedmen artisans who were their descendants.[99]

Although many goldsmiths appear as slaves in rich private households or in the retinue of the emperors, it is probable that such servile labor interfered with private production only to the extent of supplying the demands of a small portion of the wealthiest class and of the imperial court.[100] Illustrative of the small independent artisan's workroom, where most of the work in gold for the city was carried on, is the scene portrayed on the shop sign of an *aurifex brattiarius,* a smith whose specialty was gold leaf (VI, 9210) : [101] the craftsman is seated by an anvil on which he is pounding out the gold with a rather heavy hammer; a scale to weigh the gold hangs nearby on the wall. On the tomb of another worker, a specialist in chased ware—both silver and gold (VI, 9149), the complete tools of the trade are portrayed: a scale, a sharp-edged engraving tool, a compass, plates of gold leaf, and one of the

---

[98] *C. I. L.,* III, 8839, Dalmatia: a *te[re]utice[n]sis ab urbe.*

[99] According to Gummerus (278) there were 33 independent artisans (plus 11 not certain) and 2 freeborn (plus 4 not certain) of Greek or Eastern extraction engaged in this work.

[100] Gummerus, 282.

[101] Published by Jahn, "Darstellungen antiker Reliefs welche sich auf Handwerk und Handelsverkehr beziehen," *Berichte der königlich-sächsischen Gesell. der Wissenschaften,* XIII (1861), pl. 7, 2.

finished products—a golden wreath.[102] From passages in the jurists it appears that such craftsmen worked under varied conditions. At times, the goldsmiths owned their raw materials (*Dig.*, 19, 5, 20, 2); at others, it was furnished by the patron for whom the craftsmen worked as *institores*;[103] on still other occasions, the customers brought their own materials.[104] This last method seems, moreover, to have been the most usual. Small commissions might even be given to an itinerant artisan, who pounded out a ring or a bracelet on his well-worn anvil before the eyes of the curious crowd (Mart., 12, 57, 9).

The existence of two guilds of goldsmiths offers additional testimony to the prevalence of small craft shops: a group of *aurifices* is known for the time of Augustus, when a freedman from Asia Minor, A. Fourius A. l. Seleucus, was its president (VI, 9202); and the *collegium* of gilders and workers in gold leaf *brattiarii inauratores* can also be dated in this period (VI, 95).

The booths of individual members of these groups were scattered throughout the city: *de Sacra Via* (VI, 9207 and *Eph. Ep.*, IX, 438), *de Vico Longo* (VI, 37469), *a Lacu Gallinae* (33835), *extra Portam Flumentanam* (VI, 9208), and *de Aurelianis* (*A. J. A.,* XII [1908], 45). Because records of these shops have survived in unusual numbers it is possible to trace connections between the various artisans. For example, a free citizen of the late republic, M'. Obellius M'. f. Vo....., owned a goldsmith's shop on the Sacred Street, and in the first century A. D. the tombstone of a M'. Obellius Acastus records the fact that he had been a worker in gold *de Aurelianis* (*hortis* or *horreis*). The conclusion is perhaps not unwarranted that Acastus had been a slave of the free citizen who had learned his trade assisting his master; after his manumission he had established his own shop. The

---

[102] Amelung, *Die Skulpturen des Vatikanischen Museums*, I, 247.
[103] For example, *C. I. L.*, VI, 9222: here a wealthy patron had equipped the artisan's shop. See also *C. I. L.*, X, 3948 (Bruns, 370-1), where the patron of an artisan rents out his services for a period of time at a fixed rate.
[104] Sulpicius Rufus in *Dig.*, 19, 2, 31; see also 34, 2, 34; 19, 2, 2, 1; etc., and Diocletian's edict.

records of the freedmen of A. Septicius show an apprentice-
ship system of like nature and possibly an unusual scale of
production.[105]

There was also a great need for intaglios and cameos to
fit in the rings and bracelets made by the goldsmiths, and the
gemmarii named so frequently in the inscriptions were the
craftsmen who met this demand. Only one artisan in the city
is actually called a *gemmarius sculptor* (VI, 9436); so the
usual assumption is that the other *gemmarii* were primarily
dealers. But at that stage of industrial development where the
small artisan and sales shop is the leading method of production, it is unnatural to draw the fine line that separates
the merchant from the workman. Consequently, M. Lollius
Alexander, the *gemmarius* who had prospered in his trade to
the extent of erecting a temple (VI, 9433), may have been
either a large dealer in imported stones (comparable to the
wealthy pearl merchants of the city)[106] or an artist whose
talent and remunerations were comparable to the engravers of
the famous frog of Maecenas or the portrait of Augustus.[107]
The most interesting group of these dealers, or rather artists,
are the five *gemari* (*sic*) *de Sacra Via* (VI, 9435). Since
there are three freedmen of Q. Plotius and a freedman and a

---

[105] A Greek freedman, A. Septicius A. l. Apollonius, and his wife,
Septicia A. l. Rufa, were workers in gold leaf (VI, 6939). There
was also a *de sacra via auri aceptor*, A. Septicius A. ⊃. l. Salvius
(9212), whose inscription is of the same date as that of Apollonius
and probably comes from the same columbarium (Gummerus, 261-2).
Consequently, it is possible that both men had worked as slaves in
the famous shop of that Septicius who originated the well-known
Septician ware (Mart., 8, 71, 6; 4, 88, 3. Although Septician ware
is here spoken of as inferior kind of silver plate, the craftsmen were
probably trained in the various metal techniques). If, as seems
likely, Septicius put his plate and probably jewelry on the market
in considerable quantities, he may have owned several branch shops
or operated a "factory" where specialists worked under one roof.
In either case, because of the need of a considerable capital this
reconstructed shop of Septicius would be rare in the city.
[106] Chap. III, 135.
[107] The name of Dioscurides, the gem cutter who produced the portrait (Pl., 37, 8 and 10), appears on numerous extant gems, though
ten are generally regarded as his work (Rossbach, " Dioskurides,"
no. 16 in *P.-W.*, V, 1143). This artist of high rank, an immigrant
from the East, had no need of a shop like those along the Sacred
Way.

freedwoman of C. Bobbius, some bond of union must be assumed; we may have either five or four artists working together in a single shop or five renters of contiguous booths. It is possible, too, that the ringmakers, who had been organized in a guild since the days of the republic (VI, 9144), not only made settings but carved the stones. These craftsmen had concentrated on the *Scalae Anulariae* near the Forum (Suet., *Aug.*, 72).[108]

Silver. Silverware from Campanian factories, which was exported to many parts of Europe,[109] probably came in large quantities to the capital; accordingly, the successive styles of silver plate that had been produced in sufficiently large quantities to have won a special trade name—the Furian, Clodian, and Gratian—may have originated there.[110] Strangely enough, however, there are inscriptions of Clodii and Furii who worked in silver at Rome: P. Clodius P. l. Dida, a *vascularius* (VI, 9955), and L. Furius L. l. Diomedes, a *caelator de Sacra Via* (9221). If we may infer from such slim evidence that these artists represent freedmen of the original Clodius [111] or Furius, Pliny's three styles originated here. That " Clodian " or " Furian " in Pliny's time was a title applied to a style and not to the products of the large

---

[108] Among the makers of special articles of jewelry known from the inscriptions, the young slave Pagus, put out as an apprentice at the age of twelve to learn the art of decorating gold bracelets with precious stone, had the shortest career and the most moving epitaph (VI, 9437).

[109] The plate found at Pompeii in all likelihood came from Campanian shops (Frank, *Econ. Hist.*, 253). Gummerus ("Die röm. Industrie," 260) declares that the Hildesheim treasure was made in Italy and that the extraordinarily fine mirror in the Boscoreale trove with the signature of M. Domitius Polygnos was made in Italy, possibly near Pompeii. For details of technique see Maiuri, *La Casa del Menandro e il suo tresoro di argenteria*, 1933, 241-385.

[110] Pl., 33, 139. Martial (4, 39, 6), moreover, speaks of *vera Gratiana*, implying that the popular ware was imitated.

[111] Van Buren ("Antiquities of the Janiculum," *Memoirs of the American Academy in Rome*, XI [1933], 73-8) suggests other related workers: Clodia Cypare named on the inscription of an *aurifex* (VI, 9207), C. Clodius Fausti l. Felix, *ad margarita[s]* (9543), and P. Clodius Proculus, a *figulus* of Arretine ware ("Clodius," no. 47 in *P.-W.*, IV, 82). Proculus could use the technique learned in the original silver plate manufactory to produce moulds for clay vessels.

factory is proved by the inscription of M. Canuleius Zosimus, (VI, 9222) : Zosimus, a freedman who worked for the account of his patron, was at the age of twenty-eight a master of the *caelatura Clodiana.* In that case the assumption of large-scale production even in the original shops rests on the postulate that the plate captured the market because of the amounts in which it was produced rather than because of its fine workmanship.

Nevertheless, since division of labor in the making of silver plate had appeared in Campania,[112] it is necessary to search for evidence of its existence among the artisans at Rome. From the urban inscriptions the following specialists can be enumerated: *caelatores,* engravers (VI, 9222, 9432, 37750, 9239); *inaurator,* a decorator who adds the touches of gold (VI, 3928); *tritor argentarius,* a polisher (VI, 9950); *toreuticensis,* an embosser (III, 8839, *ab urbe*); and *flaturarii,* casters (VI, 9418-9). At a much later age the implication of the varied skills contained in such names becomes a definite statement (Augustine, *de Civitate Dei,* 7, 4): *vel tamquam opifices in vico argentario ubi unum vasculum ut perfectum exeat per multos artifices transit cum ab uno perfecto perfici posset.* There are, moreover, among the inscriptions of *fabri argentari* and *vasculari* indications of large units of workers. Though five freedmen of a C. Junius are designated as "silversmiths" (VI, 9391), there is no way of distinguishing whether each smith was a master workman completing an entire piece of work or whether he labored with his fellow freedmen on one elaborate bowl. Again, A. Fulvius A. l. Dorotheus, a *vascularius* of the early empire (VI, 33919), has engraved on his tombstone the names of nineteen freedmen and women. The conclusion that Fulvius operated a silver plate manufactory is, of course, dangerous;[113] nevertheless, the existence of such groups of workers accords with a theory of large-scale production, a system that is known to have

---

[112] See Frank, *Econ. Hist.,* 253-4.

[113] One of the freedwomen named in the group is probably Dorotheus' mother, and the others may be merely fellow freedmen. If this is an artisan group, however, it is the largest known from the inscriptions of the ancient city.

existed elsewhere and is supported by the presence of specialized workers in the city.

Although we may probably assume that some silverware was
produced in larger shops, over thirty inscriptions testify to
the activities of the individual craftsman. It is likely that
some of them were concentrated in the Sigillaria, where the
ill-starred silver chariot was destroyed by the censors before
the eyes of the prospective purchasers (Suet., *Claud.*, 16).
The silversmith Curtilius Hermeros, who became *magister
vici ab Cyclopis* (VI, 2226), undoubtedly had his shop in the
district of the antrum Cyclopis. His election to the position
of district manager, as well as the names of freedmen on his
epitaph, proves that he had found his calling profitable.
Another story of success among these independent silversmiths can be read from the two inscriptions concerned with
the former slaves of P. Durdenus.[114]

Copper and Iron. Since copper and bronze articles from
Capuan workrooms were exported to Rome in considerable
quantities, it is likely that some of the urban *aerarii* were primarily distributors. In most cases, however, they must have
combined the functions of craftsmen and salesmen, as it was
customary for petty artisans at work in small shops to make
on order pots, kettles, and bowls, often melting down an
article of stock to supply material for immediate needs.[115]
Several varieties of workers in bronze are also named in the
inscriptions: there are *sigillarii* (makers of small statuettes

---

[114] Eros, in all likelihood a *vascularius*, set up a tablet to his
brother and patron, a member of the guild of silversmiths connected
with the imperial palace (VI, 9952). Later we find their sister
(daughter or freedwoman), Durdena P. l. Cytheris, married to a
freedman engaged in the same trade as the brothers (VI, 1818). In
the next generation her son attained the relatively important position of secretary to the quaestors. His father's wealth, to which
the freedmen on the tombstone bear eloquent testimony, had obviously
helped Flaccus in his rise, and perhaps it is not incorrect to assume
as its source a large shop or even manufactory.

[115] Then, too, Martial complains of the clatter of the coppersmiths'
mallets, which, beginning at an early hour, continued throughout
the day (9, 68, 5-6; see also Juv., 7, 223 ff.); and there is always
Horace's famous *Aemilium circa ludum faber imus* (*Ep.*, 2, 3, 2-3;
Porphyrio [ed. Holder] declares the gladiatorial school of Aemilius
Lepidus had shops *in angulo*).

[?]: VI, 9894-5), *aerari statuarii* (makers of bronze and copper statuary: 9137), and *erari vasclari* (sic!) (makers of bronze bowls: 9138). On the tombstone of two workers of this latter group the finished cantharos is pictured among the tools of the trade—the ladle, the blowpipe, the smith's pincers, and the anvil. In addition, between the portraits of the two workmen, A. Antestius A. l. Antiochus and A. Antestius A. l. Nicia, the wife of one appears. Because of the fine features of the woman's face (her name was Rufa) it has been suggested that she was the daughter of the former patron of the freedman who had brought her father's workshop to one of them as a dowry.[116] Small shops of this nature are the only type of production mentioned in the inscriptions, and the presence of numerous individual workers is further proved by the existence of a *conlegium aerariorum* from the period of the late republic (VI, 36771).

The fact that the *flaturarii* in two inscriptions (VI, 9418 and 9419) name the location of their workrooms (*de via Sacra*) may establish them as independent workers engaged in casting bronze for state money. Part of this money we know was prepared by the imperial slaves belonging to the *familia monetalis,* but some of it—especially the casting of the blanks—was let out to private entrepreneurs.[117] Valuable, though indirect, information about the type of workmen selected to fulfil such contracts is given by the inscription of P. Monetius Soc. l. Philogenes (9953: early empire) who is called a *vascularius.* According to Mommsen's note in the *Corpus,* the *socii* or *societas,* whose slave Philogenes had been, were the *conductores* who leased the right to strike the copper nummus, and it is likely that Philogenes had learned his trade from these contractors, themselves skilled craftsmen in bronze. Other inscriptions recording imperial freedmen (VI, 8452) or large contractors engaged in making cop-

---

116 Gummerus, "Darstellungen," 75.

117 Mattingly (*Roman Coins,* 1928, 133-4) states that even in Trajan's time no more than a couple of hundred men at most were directly employed by the state in the preparation of money. For private work see, for example, *C. I. L.,* VI, 8455 and XIV, 3642.

per money (9455) give no evidence of the type of shop or of
any accessory artistic activities.

Perhaps the importers of armor and heavy farm instruments from Puteoli brought smaller articles of iron to the
city dealers from this source,[118] but inscriptions of smiths,
lock makers, and nail makers in the capital prove that implements of daily use were made to order.[119] The famous altar
of L. Cornelius Atimetus in the Vatican Gallery [120] and the
tombstone of the worker in iron from the Isola Sacra [121]
offer clear-cut evidence of the products and the method of
local Roman industry. In the workshop pictured on the
left face of the altar two men are engaged in beating out a
piece of iron on an anvil. Above their heads on a stand are
hung the finished articles: a broad sacrificial knife, a vine-
dresser's knife, a pair of pincers, and a triangular piece of
iron with a cutting edge. In the shop pictured on the right,
Atimetus is showing a prospective buyer his wares; these,
displayed to some advantage in a three-shelved cupboard,
consist of sickles, garden knives, butcher knives, the same
triangular cutting edges, and cases of five sharp-pointed instruments. The fact that Atimetus had a special salesroom
shows that he was unusually prosperous; but even here there
are no indications of anything beyond the small-shop system.

In the only inscription which mentions the guild of *fabri
ferrarii* (VI, 1892) an important member of the " senate "
is named: M. Sutorius M. l. Pamphilus, a lictor in the
service of the priests who performed the public sacrifices and
an aide to the consul and praetor. It would seem that such
public duties enabled Pamphilus to spend little time at his
forge; since, however, three freedmen and several freedwomen are found on his epitaph, they were probably the ones
who carried on the work of the shop. It is not likely that
ordinary members of the guild had workrooms of comparable

---

[118] The *negotiatores ferrarii* (Chap. I, n. 154).
[119] *Clavarius* (key maker: *C.I.L.*, VI, 9259), *clostrarius* (lock-
smith: VI, 9260), *cultrarii* (cutlers: I, 1213), etc.
[120] VI, 16166; reproduced in Amelung, I, 275-7.
[121] See *N. S.*, 1931, 536. In addition to spits, knives, and shears,
an anvil and an iron bedstead are pictured among the products of
the shop.

size, though there is a record of one large group of *ferrarii de F.* (VI, 9398) consisting of two freedmen patrons and their five freedmen.[122]

VII. HOUSEHOLD FURNISHINGS

Glassware. While the rich drank from goblets of Egyptian and Sidonian crystal or ate from embossed Capuan silver, the poor were satisfied with the clay dishes made on the Vatican (Juv., 6, 344; cf. Mart., 1, 18, 2; 12, 48, 4, *et passim*) or the cheap urban goblets with their long beakers like Vatinius' nose (Mart., 14, 96; 10, 3, 4). Pottery from the factories at Arretium and later in Gaul also appeared on many Roman tables, but the cruder *amphorae, pelves,* and *dolia* were produced in the brickyards close to the city.[123] The scales of production in this ware will be considered in a discussion of the brick industry. Furthermore, in the time of Augustus, the city became the centre for the manufacturing of the fine black " Medaillonschalen " and later of the false sigillata of the second century.[124]

Since the sand at the mouth of the Tiber was dark and far inferior to the brilliant white sand of the Volturnus, we may assume that little glass was produced at Rome during the early years of the empire. Fine sand in sufficient quantities could only be imported with difficulty, for the sand from the Anio, even in its upper courses, was not particularly suitable. There is a notice in Strabo about glassware at Rome,

---

[122] This, the largest group of smiths known from the city, is composed of T. Titus T. Ͻ. l. S... and T. Titus T. l. Spinicus, their wives, and five freedmen. It is difficult to imagine these freedmen working at their individual anvils (and no other method of production was known in the Roman world) within the confines of a single room. Like the *falcarii* concentrated on a single street in Cicero's day or the artisans who were probably gathered in the *Vicus* ....-*ionum Ferrariarum* (VI, 9185) they may have worked in several contiguous booths. Furthermore, the possibility exists that these Greeks were not workmen but dealers in imported wares; the *scutarius* (VI, 9886), the *cassidarii* (1952), and the *gladiarius* (9442) may also have retailed articles that had been made elsewhere.

[123] Roman *pelves*, a specialty of some brick factories at Rome, have been found in Pompeii, Etruria, and northern Italy (Gummerus, *P.-W.*, 1471).

[124] Pagenstecher, *Die calenische Reliefkeramik*, 1909, 176 ff.

on the other hand,[125] which has led many to conclude that the workshops of certain Syrian artists, whose mould-blown ware has been found at the capital, were located on the spot.[126] The numerous thumb-plate handles stamped with the name of Artas which are extant in the western provinces seemed to add special weight to the assumption.   Now, however, Artas ware is generally regarded as an import.[127]   Even the branch workshop of Ennion, formerly located at Rome, belongs rather down the coast at Cumae or Liternum.[128]

Granted that Rome did not become a centre for glass blowing, there was some production, if only the mending and re-melting of broken articles.   Martial (1, 41, 3-4) speaks of the hawker who collected bits of broken glass; [129] and the Vicus Vitrarius, in existence at Rome in the fourth century (*Curiosum*, Reg. I), may have served as the glass makers' quarters at a much earlier date.[130]   The *vitric*(*ius*), M. Clodius M. l. Posidonius (VI, 7547), probably lived on this street along with the *specularii*, craftsmen who worked in mica or isinglass (VI, 9899, 9900, 33911).[131]   A specialist in this *ars specularia*, Sabinus Santias (33911: third or fourth

---

[125] Str., 16, 2, 25: "And at Rome also it is said that many discoveries are made both for producing the colors and for facility in manufacturing, as for example, in the case of glassware where one can buy a glass beaker or a drinking cup for a copper." "The facility in manufacturing" undoubtedly refers to the discovery of the blowpipe, with which the molten glass was forced into hollow moulds, thus making possible production on a large scale (Kisa, *Das Glas im Altertume*, 696).

[126] Gummerus, *P.-W.*, 1465-6, 1471, 1478-9; Kisa, 702; Dressel in *C.I.L.*, XV, 6957-9 with notes to 6958.

[127] Harden ("Romano-Syrian Glasses with Mould-Blown Inscriptions," *J.R.S.*, XXV [1935], 163-186, especially 180) concludes that most of the Sidonian glass was made in the East.   See also Heichelheim, "Roman Syria," *Economic Survey*, IV, 1938, 189 ff.; Rostovtzeff, *Storia econ.*, Chap. V, n. 43; *P.-W.*, "Artas."

[128] Harden (*ibid.*) suggests that Ennion's cups were made in Italy. Both Heichelheim (*ibid.*) and Kisa (704) believe he had transferred his business from Sidon to Rome.   The city undoubtedly offered a large market for expensive articles of glass.

[129] See also Stat., 1, 6, 74; Pl., 36, 199.

[130] Cf. the Clivus Vitriarius at Puteoli (*Eph. Ep.*, VIII, 365).   A portico among the glass-blowers may also be referred to in VI, 29844 (Trowbridge, *Philological Studies in Ancient Glass*, reprinted from *Univ. of Illinois Studies*, XIII, nos. 3 and 4 [1930], 66).

[131] The *lagunar*(*ia*) *ad Porta Trig*(*emina*) (VI, 9488) was either a dealer in bottles or a bottle maker.   Cf. the *lagonarius* (37807).

century), showed by the diagram on his tombstone that he was a maker of window panes, but has left no indication of the material used.[132] There was, moreover, a guild of *specularii* (2206) : possibly mirror-makers, as Waltzing assumes,[133] or possibly workers in glass or mica. At all events, it is fairly certain that the *specularii* in the private households had something to do with glassware, if only to repair or to clean imported crystal.[134]

Furniture. In the first chapter the evidence pointing toward the importation of furniture from factories at Ostia and Pompeii was considered and also the supply of ivory and citrus wood available for cabinetmakers and specialists in woodwork at Rome. It was even suggested that the important guild of *negotiatores eborarii et citrarii* was composed of the craftsmen who manufactured the extraordinarily expensive intarsia tables described by Pliny or executed other commissions of well-to-do customers.[135] The members of the large carpenters' guilds who carried on the building activities of the capital, especially those in the *collegium fabrum intestinariorum,* could certainly devote part of their time to producing the simple wooden tables and chests in common use. In addition, there are extant inscriptions of craftsmen who specialized in litters (VI, 7882, *faber lectarius*), flutes (935, *tibiarius*), and bookcases (9885, *scriniarius*). Probably part of the work of the three *eborarii* (7655, 9375, 37793) was to prepare carved legs for citrus tables or the ivory inlay that decorated many of the frames.[136]

In a scene from a cabinetmaker's shop preserved on a sarcophagus from the third century, the master craftsman himself is shown at his joiner's bench carving a table leg, the top of which is shaped like a lion's head and the base like that of a claw. Nearby is a helper using a hammer and plane.[137]

---

[132] Traces of glass windows from ancient times have been found: Blümner, " Glas," *P.-W.*, VII, 1388-9; Kisa, 362; Sen., *Ep.*, 90, 25.
[133] IV, 44; also Trowbridge, 66-7.
[134] VI, 8659-60; 7297, 7299, 9044, etc.
[135] Chap. I, 49. See also Waltzing, I, 218; II, 451 and Mau, " Eborarii," *P.-W.*, V, 1898.
[136] See Richter, *Ancient Furniture,* 148-158.
[137] Jahn, pl. 10, 1.

Another furniture shop, pictured on a decorated glass bowl of the Christian era, reveals six specialists working together in a miniature "factory" system: the central figure carrying the roll is evidently the owner of the establishment; to his left one man works with a bow and drill, another with a saw, and still another with an ax. To the right a craftsman is splitting wood with a chisel and hammer, while a second is carefully cutting out a carved leg and a third is finishing off a bit of metal decoration.[138] Here is definite evidence of a rather elaborate division of labor; and it is likely that the need for specialized workers in wood, in metal, and in ivory created numerous similar shops for the production of fine furniture in the city.

The discovery of a new inscription of a *glutinarius,* a freedman of Publius Clodius, has aroused speculation about the industrial activities in the household of his patron.[139] *Glutinarii* are rare in the inscriptions; the only two known from Rome are P. Clodius P. l. Metrodorus (VI, 9448) and this P. Clodius P. l. Diophanes. These specialists were makers of the glue needed in the treatment of paper, in bookmaking, in the joiner's work, and in ivory inlay.[140] Since it also happens that the record of another freedman of P. Clodius, a worker in ivory, has survived (VI, 9375), it seems probable that the three former slaves had been making articles with ivory inlay in the furniture factory of Clodius. Its size is indicated to some degree by the existence of two glue makers (or gluers) for approximately the same period. At the time of their death the two *glutinarii* have freedmen of their own, probably working with them on a partnership basis. At the death of their patron, or when they had accumulated enough capital to buy the expensive raw materials,[141] these freedmen also may have set up independent shops. Some apprentice system of this nature was essential for the

---

[138] *Ibid.,* pl. 11, 1.
[139] Van Buren, *Memoirs of the American Academy at Rome,* XI (1933), 73-8 and *Ancient Rome,* 116-17.
[140] Perhaps they were also "gluers"; see Blümner, I, 318 ff.
[141] Prices of tables made from citrus wood and ivory are given by Pliny (13, 92-3): Cicero paid $50,000 for one; Cethegus, $65,000; and the table of Juba sold at auction for $60,000.

preservation of the trade secrets in the various branches of artistic work.

VIII. LARGER MANUFACTORIES

In the making of luxury furniture the need for trained artisans in specialized fields made the aggregation of a body of workers desirable and profitable. In breadmaking, tanning, and fulling the need of expensive equipment was found to have fostered the same result. Furthermore, in the days of the early empire at Rome there were additional circumstances aiding the growth of manufactories of some size: slaves were available in large number and capital had been accumulated in the hands of the upper class.[142] The operation of these forces can be observed most profitably in three Roman industries where remains are available for defining the scale of work: the making of bricks, clay lamps, and lead pipes.

Two Roman " Factories." As a preliminary to the consideration of this evidence two references to " factories " at Rome in the sources, rare in Latin literature, demand attention. In the case of the " factory " for producing " Pompeian red " (*minium*), however, the method of production is also of some intrinsic importance because of the inferences that may be drawn in regard to the products from other state-owned properties which were directed to Rome. Vitruvius (7, 9, 3-4) gives the steps in the complicated method of preparation: first the quicksilver was collected out of the ore by a drying process and next the dried ore was crushed and washed for the vermilion color. Then he says of the Roman shops:

---

[142] The business manager (usually a freedman) of a wealthy senator could quietly invest the surplus derived from his estates in industrial enterprises, but risks were great in the absence of corporation laws. Producers of Arretine ware, of Capuan bronze, and of Campanian silverware were unusual in Roman society. There is slight evidence, moreover, that any of the large fortunes mentioned by Pliny (33, 133-5) came from industry, though C. Caecilius C. l. Isidorus (who had 4116 slaves and 60 million sesterces) may have accumulated his wealth from business undertakings. The profits to be made by setting up slaves in business are discussed more fully under *institores* (Chap. III).

The workshops (*officinae*) which were in the Ephesian mines are now removed to Rome, because this kind of vein has been discovered in parts of Spain. The ore from the Spanish mines is conveyed to Rome and dealt with by the publicans. The workshops are between the temples of Flora and Quirinus.[143]

Additional details from Pliny (33, 118) complete the picture. From these state-owned mines at Sisapo (Almaden) 2,000 lbs. of ore, in a crude state and under seal, were sent each year to the city. The mining, shipping, and manufacturing were left in the hands of the *publicani* who rented the mines, but the sales price was regulated by law so as not to exceed 70 sesterces a pound.[144]   In addition to these passages, an inscription has preserved the name of the procurator of the company for the early years of Augustus.[145]

Since *minium* was used not only by potters, fullers, doctors, and artists but demanded by the ritualistic state worship and on certain public celebrations, interest on the part of the government in controlling the price was to be expected. Further, because of the scarcity of the supply this publican society enjoyed a monopoly of the mineral.   Under such conditions the measures adopted by the state cannot be taken as indicative of the treatment of other public products sent to Rome.   The interest of the government, however, in the sale of state materials is worthy of notice.[146]

The other manufactory is known to us only from a passage in Pliny (13, 75-6).   In the time of Augustus a certain Fannius had established at Rome a workroom where the third grade of Egyptian papyrus was reprocessed and made into the finest quality paper.   The account, which incidentally

---

[143] On the Quirinal: see Lanciani, *Forma Urbis Romae*, pl. 16, and *B. C.*, XVII (1889), 384 f.

[144] Kroll ("Minium," *P.-W.*, XV², 1848) declares that it is possible that Pliny had access to the "Mitteilungen von Händlern."

[145] C. Miniarius Atimetus (a former slave of the publicans) is now *procurator sociorum miniariarum* (VI, 9634).   The same company may be referred to in the tablet (*A. J. A.*, XVI [1912], 94) set up by C. Clodius C. f. Magnus and C. Clodius Crescens *argentarius* to the *pigmentarii et miniarii*.

[146] The state also enjoyed a monopoly in sulphur from Sicily (Pl., 35, 174), in alum from Sicily (*ibid.*, 184), and in nitre from Egypt (31, 46).   Because of the bulk of these minerals it is not likely that they, like *minium*, were refined at Rome, though the state may have supervised the shipment to the capital and the sale there.

makes it clear that the production of papyrus remained exclusively in Egypt, runs as follows:

> The skilful *officina* that was established by Fannius at Rome was in the habit of receiving the last kind (the lowest grade, called *amphitheatrica*) and there, by a very careful process of insertion, of rendering it much finer. So much so, that from being a common sort, he made it into a paper of first-rate quality and gave his own name to it.[147]

No indications of the size of the shop are given, but Pliny's interest in it implies that Fannius' "factory" was both important and unusual.

Brickmaking. Because of the detailed information on Roman brick stamps the clearest conception of large-scale production in the city can be formed for this industry.[148] On the stamps appear the names of the owner of the estate on which the kilns were located, of the manager of the kiln, of the maker of the tile, and the consular date. All these items do not, of course, appear on every brick; yet from the available information it is possible not only to reconstruct the size of the shops in which this important building material was produced, but even to watch the gradual and almost accidental concentration of the yards into the hands of members of the imperial family.

The capital city offered to this industry a constant large market, and the surrounding soil, generous deposits of satisfactory clay. The great suburban estates in the valley of the Tiber, where soil of good alluvial origin existed along with pozzolano (which when pulverized tempered the excessive plasticity of the clay), had been from the first the centres of production; there, many of the rich landowners had engaged

---

[147] Wünsch, "Charta," *P.-W.*, III, 2185-92, especially 2189. This cheap grade, useful only for wrappings, was changed by Fannius into a wider paper named Fanniana.

[148] Dressel's collection in *C.I.L.*, XV¹, 1891, must of necessity form the basis of this discussion. Cozzo ("Una industria nella Roma imperiale. La corporazione dei figuli ed i bolli doliari," *Mem. Acc. Lin.*, 1936, 233-366) has added some of the new finds and grouped the inscriptions chronologically, but his conclusions are unusual and often unsound. In his *Ingegneria Romana* (133-148) he has also treated the use and production of bricks. Gummerus, "Industrie und Handel," *P.-W.*, 1485-7, has based his conclusions on Dressel's collection.

willingly in an industry which, since it was originally a branch
of farm work, had been free from the stigma attached to
other industrial pursuits.[149] Though clay was abundant all
along the river, the product was too heavy for ready transport and it was easy for a few estates near the city to gain
control of production.[150] Some of these are known by name:
the famous Salerenses on the Via Salaria (*C. I. L.*, XV,
478 f.) and the kilns on the Viae Nomentana (XV, 677-82),
Aurelia (672), and Triumphalis (684).

During the republic there was little demand for brick; even
in the building program of Caesar tufa and travertine still
formed the usual materials for facings.[151] For small houses
sundried brick had been used early, but it was not until
Augustus' time that the concrete walls of public buildings were
faced with irregularly shaped fragments of roof tiles. Later,
with the advance in technical skill under Claudius, triangular
bricks supplanted this facing of sherds. In Nero's time, however, especially after the great fire of 64 when vast amounts of
fireproof material for building were needed, the brick industry came into its own.[152] The Flavian building program
kept alive the demand; and if we can judge from the number
of remaining bricks that bear the consular stamp, under
Hadrian a peak in production was reached. Then with the
accession of Antoninus Pius and Marcus Aurelius, who as
private citizens had inherited the most productive brickyards

---

[149] Jars for the storage of farm products had always been made
on suburban estates, and later *dolia, amphorae, pelves, arcae,* and
even *sarcophagi* continued to be produced in the brickyards. *Pelves*
from the kilns of the two Domitii were at Pompeii before 79 A. D.,
and *amphorae* produced near the city reached Aquae Sextiae (XV,
2483) and Clusium (2484).

[150] Campanian, Ligurian, and Gallic bricks found at Rome's seaport came as ballast. Brickyards on the Tiber even 100 miles above
Rome, however, gained a market down the river. For instance,
bricks from the Tusculan estate of Annia Arescusa (XV, 2226) and
from the estate belonging to Plotilla and the father of Nerva in the
Praenestine fields (2341) have been found in the city. Such importation, however, was not usual.

[151] See Van Deman, "Methods of Determining the Date of Roman
Concrete Monuments," *A. J. A.*, XVI (1912), 230-251 and 387-432.

[152] Cozzo ("Una industrie," 244-5) shows that the increased height
of the houses and the floods of 54 emphasized the need for baked
brick.

near the city, the factories formed a part of the imperial *res privata*. Finally, as a result of a change in dynasty these private properties became part of the imperial estate, to which were added the yards of rich citizens which Severus confiscated in great numbers. By the time of the building of the Thermae Antoninianae (212-13 A. D.) the making of bricks, through the process of inheritance, was practically a state monopoly.

Since the yards that had been inherited by the Emperor Marcus Aurelius had belonged originally to the gens Domitia, the growth of the factories of this family offers a significant cross-section of the development of the industry at Rome.[153] The founder, Cn. Domitius Afer, the famous orator from Nîmes, had at the time of his death in 59 A. D.—according to Dressel's calculations—approximately three freedmen foremen and six slaves at work in his yards. In 59, when the two heirs Tullus and Lucanus took over the yards, new kilns were established and the size of production greatly enlarged. By 94 A. D., the date of Lucanus' death, the names of twenty-three slaves and five freedmen are known from bricks made in the brothers' yards. In this year many faithful slave workers were rewarded with their freedom: some of them were promoted to the position of foreman in the main yards, while others with their own or borrowed capital started to operate independent kilns.

The elder Domitia Lucilla, who, as daughter of Lucanus and adopted daughter of Tullus, came into possession of the yards in 108, founded a new branch factory, the Fulvianae.[154] Since her name is identical with that of her daughter, the wife of Annius Verus, it is impossible to distinguish the bricks made in the yards of these two women and so to trace the growth of the factories under her ownership. At the death of the younger Lucilla, however, six years before her son Marcus came to the throne, the names of nineteen slaves and of twenty-seven freedmen employed in her kilns are known from the bricks. Most

---

[153] The details have been worked out by Dressel, 268 ff.
[154] Before that time there had been four main divisions: the Caninianae, Terentianae, Caepionianae, and Licinianae.

of these forty-six men, in general native-born Italians, represent foremen of individual pits. By this time also there were imperial freedmen managing sections of the Domitian yards.

After Marcus Aurelius became emperor the bricks of the Domitian yards were stamped Aug Ñ. The difficulty of determining whether Marcus or a later emperor is designated by that formula and the use of the name M. Aurelius Antoninus by Caracalla make any further calculations highly uncertain. We know, however, that the yards in the possession of Marcus, inherited from his mother and father—as well as from Pius, C. Curiatius Cosanus, and T. Tutinius Sentius Sabinus—included fourteen *figlinae*.[155] Since, however, approximately forty smaller yards continued to be operated by private citizens, there is not the slightest evidence of an aggressive personal monopoly on the part of the emperors at this time.

The several thousand brick stamps classified by Dressel give but the barest hint of the tremendous size of the industry; on most of these stamps, moreover, only the name of the foreman of the kiln appears, and the number of workingmen under his control is conjectural.[156] Rather definite evidence of the number of slaves under a single foreman, however, comes from the story of the rise of a slave *figulus* who had worked for the two Domitii. Agathobulus, one of the twenty-odd foremen of the brothers, had had two fellow slaves as his helpers; later after his own manumission he freed these two also; thus his slave Trophimus became Cn. Domitius Trophimus (XV, 1112-14). Finally, Trophimus became a foreman and had four slave *figuli* under his supervision. Since a brick has been found marked *Abascanti Cn. Domiti Trophimi* (1115), it

---

[155] Caepionianae, Caninianae, Domitianae, Faurianae, Fulvianae, Germanicae, Licinianae, Mucianae, Oceanae, Ponticulanae, Pot-(   ), Publilianae, Sef(   ), and Terentianae.
[156] The importance of some of these managers and the extent of their control are shown by the change of the name of the Figlinae Marcianae (Trajan's property) to Favorianae in honor of a successful foreman, C. Calpetanus Favor (XV, 312-16). Another freedman who became a rich factory owner was T. Flavius Agathyrsus, to whom Faustina, wife of Trajan, had bequeathed one-third interest in the Figlinae Quintianae. Ten years after her death, Agathyrsus was in possession of all the kilns.

is possible that Trophimus, having established his own kiln, was able to employ his own helpers.

On about ten stamps of a later period the word *negotiatore* (or *negotiatione*), usually preceded by a woman's name, appears.[157] Gummerus is certainly correct in declaring that the word is a synonym for *conductrix* and that we are dealing here with lessees who carried on trade in their own products.[158] Cozzo's contention that there is a distinction between the *conductrix* who is interested only in production and the *negotiatrix* concerned entirely with distribution—an indication of the intense development of the industry [159]—is contrary to the testimony of the juridical sources and the whole practice of Roman industrial enterprise. Moreover, there was no stigma attached to the position of lessee, and women of position often filled it: seventeen names of such women occur on Roman bricks (three uncertain), often with the defining phrase *ex conductione* or *ex officina*.

There is clear evidence in this industry of an immense number of yards employing hundreds of workmen. Raw material was close at hand, little mechanical equipment was needed, and the building programs of the government stimulated production. In addition, because of the bulkiness and cheapness of the product, there was no question of importation from other localities. Such a combination of favoring circumstances could not be operative in many industries. Even here, however, the individual units were small, and the development of the industry resulted in more—not larger —groups.

---

[157] The names of women occur with such frequency on the brick stamps that consideration must be given to their place in the industry. Of course, many of them were owners of estates who rented out the working of clay pits located thereon to entrepreneurs; others like the two Domitiae and the famous Julia Procula took some interest in production. Julia Procula, a Greek from Mytilene who had assumed the Latin name of her patron, owned two important yards—the Sulpicianae (XV, 587) and the Tonneianae (XV, 646-51). (For further details see Cozzo, "Una industrie," 355-6.) The stamp on one of her bricks (649), which reads *tegula doliare de fig. Juliae Proculae flu(viatili) neg(otiatione)* and is decorated with the wreathed head of the river god, may point to traffic with bricks up the Tiber.

[158] *P.-W.*, 1485.   [159] *Loc. cit.*, 356.

The Production of Clay Lamps. These same deposits of good clay made Rome, together with Modena in Cisalpine Gaul and Campania, an important Italian centre for the making of clay lamps. Again the cheapness of the product necessitated local manufacturing; but for a certain period in the early first century A. D. there was an extensive exportation of Roman lamps to every part of the empire.[160] Yet, an attempt to use the abundant finds in the city to determine the scale of production is beset with numerous difficulties. In the first place, Dressel's publication in the *Corpus* includes only lamps with inscriptions, and it is a well-known fact that Rome was the chief source of the relief lamps which usually bear no names.[161] Further, a great quantity of new finds, often still unclassified, has been added to the already bulky material.[162] In the third place, there is absolute proof that some few lamps found in the city were imported; for example, the lamps of Communis, Strobilis, and Fortis originated in Cisalpine Gaul, those of C. Junius Drac(   ) in Campania, and that of Pullaenus in Africa.

Even if we assume, however, that most of the lamps found at Rome were locally produced, it is hard to reconstruct the size of the various factories from the signatures on the lamps. The names represent the owners or *conductores* of the pro-

---

[160] Broneer, *Terracotta Lamps*, IV, Part 2 of the *Corinth Publications*, 1930, 23-6. He concludes that "local craftsmen continued to put out cheap goods for the home market, such as our type XVI, but this did not seriously affect the industry and trade of the empire, which was concentrated in the capital." This export trade, chiefly in artistic relief lamps, began under Augustus and continued until the last third of the first century. The earlier lamps of graceful shape and artistic decoration were supplanted after the time of Claudius by plain undecorated factory lamps, which continued to be exported until the time of Trajan. Then articles of local manufacture competed with Roman products (see also Loeschcke, *Lampen aus Vindonissa*, 1919, 277 ff.).

[161] See Dressel in *C. I. L.*, XV², pp. 782-4; Toutain, "Lucerna," *D.-S.*, 1332; Hug, "Lucerna," *P.-W.*, XIII², 1594; Fremersdorf, *Römische Bildlampen*, 1922, 125 ff.; Déonna, "L'Ornementation des lampes romaines," *Rev. Arch.*, XXVI (1927), 233-263; Messerschmidt, "Tragödienszenen auf römischen Lampen," *Röm. Mitt.*, XLIV (1929), 26-42.

[162] See especially the work of Fremersdorf and Loeschcke on the lamps at Vindonissa, Miltner on the lamps in Eisenstadt, and Broneer on those at Corinth.

duction units, and it is only rarely that the maker of the mould is known. An unusual case is Myro's lamps (*C.I.L.*, XV, 6213, 6227, 6251) on which the names of the two *figuli* (potters), Masculus and Clemens, appear and inscriptions which, since they refer to chariot races at Rome, apparently fix the location of the shop.[163] As the term " publica " on one of the lamps (6227) shows, Myro had also secured a contract to make the large lamps used for illumination at public festivals and games. Since one of these potters could design the matrix used in the production of hundreds of lamps required on this order, the amount of unskilled labor in the factory must have been considerably greater. More convincing evidence of large groups of workmen is offered by the number of different designs appearing on lamps found at Rome, though not necessarily of urban origin: 91 subjects occur on lamps from the shop of L. Caec. Sac., 84 from that of C. Oppius Restitutus, 51 from that of Florentinus and 43 from the shop of a L. Mar( ) Mi( ).[164]

Since, however, designs on the lamps of Annius Serapiodorus (XV, 6295, 6296) reappear on those produced by Marius Fructus (6550) and Maurus (6553), too definite conclusions should not be drawn from these numbers. The lamps from Serapiodorus' shop have been found only at Rome and at Ostia, and there in great quantities; so it is generally agreed that they were produced near the city. Either Fructus and Maurus operated branch factories connected with Serapiodorus' main factory,[165] or they had, in the absence of copyright laws, made a cheap copy of his popular moulds. This reappearance of the same subject and often of the same name on lamps that obviously originated in different shops is a frequent phenomenon and complicates any estimate of size of production.

---

[163] See Broneer's discussion (88) under Type 26; Loeschcke (277) notes that Myro's name occurs on lamps from Pompeii.

[164] Toutain, 1334. The tabulations of Toutain and Dressel must remain basic, since new studies have not been concerned with the production and use of lamps.

[165] See notes to XV, 6296. These lamps of Serapiodorus belong to the late second century, but the process under discussion was always operative.

Another method of attack is based on evidence for branch factories offered by the names of potters who had originally been slaves of the same master. For example, there are lamps signed with the names of five freedmen of L. Fabricius: Aga(thopus), Evelpistus, Heraclides, Masculus, and Saturninus. It is not improbable, as Toutain suggests,[166] that these Greeks had been designers in a large factory owned by a L. Fabricius, and that he had freed them and placed them in charge of factories connected with the main unit. To determine the size of production it would be valuable to know if the various Fabricii were contemporary; proof of this is uncertain, but the evidence is on the whole negative.[167] It is even possible, moreover, that some of these freedmen had been former slave helpers of the others, for Masculus is known to have had two *figuli*: Maximus (XV, 6250) and Pulcher (6434). The name of Maximus appears on a lamp from the shop of L. Fabricius Masculus made in honor of the famous chariot horse, Corax, who died in the time of Claudius (6250). This funeral lamp, certainly urban in origin, suggests the location of the factories of the Fabricii, though finds have been discovered in Africa and Cisalpine Gaul.

Lamps from Roman shops during the height of production in the early first century A. D. were, like the bowls from the Arretine factories, distributed to all parts of the Mediterranean. About the time of Vespasian when their artistic quality had declined and undecorated lamps became popular, the need for these cheap lamps at a minimum cost probably encouraged manufacturing in larger shops.[168] Any attempt to

---

[166] *D.-S.*, 1331. A similar group of six freedmen of a L. Munatius can be determined from finds in Rome and in Africa. It is interesting to find a Munatius Successus (the name of one potter) among the funerary inscriptions at Rome (VI, 22671).

[167] Fink, " Formen und Stempel römischer Thonlampen," *Sitzungsberichte der Kön. Bay. Ak. der Wiss. zu München*, XLVII (1900), 685-703, especially 690. Although Fink's criteria are outdated (see Hug, 1595), there is little additional information bearing on this specific problem.

[168] Fremersdorf (125) suggests that the potters' shops with their moulds were destroyed in the civil wars following the reign of Nero and that the hasty reëstablishment of the industry caused the decline in artistry. Broneer (25-26) criticizes this view, but concludes that the period of political unrest disturbed the prosperity of the upper class, which usually demanded more richly decorated lamps.

estimate the size of the production units from the inscriptions
on the lamps is of necessity unsatisfactory, but the simplicity
of the manufacturing process, the impossibility of preserving
trade secrets, and the cheapness of the raw material, must have
prevented the emergence of a few very large concerns. These
same factors by the time of Trajan resulted in the successful
competition of small local industry.

The Making of Lead Pipes. In the production of the vast
number of lead pipes through which water from the many city
aqueducts was brought to imperial palaces and public fountains, large factories run by imperial slaves would seem to be
an inevitable result of the following conditions. In the first
place, the necessary lead came directly to the city as a fiscal
product; [169] then, as Frontinus' account shows (78-87), there
was a constant demand for pipes of certain standard sizes;
further, there were two groups of imperial slaves, over 700 in
all, available for work on the aqueducts.[170]   It is true that
many of these slaves were engaged in inspection and repair
jobs (Frontinus mentions *vilici, castellani, circitores, silicarii,*
and *tectores*), but there were others who made the pipes,
aliique opifices. The actual number engaged in manufacturing is difficult to determine, but, according to the lists com-
piled by Dressel (*C. I. L.,* XV², pp. 907-8), during the fifteen
years of Domitian's rule there were ten slaves and six freedmen in charge of the shops where the pipes for imperial
structures were made.[171]

The number of slaves assisting each of these *plumbiarii*
would depend to a large extent on the nature of the manufacturing process. It was a simple one. The lead was cast into
flat sheets on a stone form, usually ten feet long, on which
were incised the names of the public official in charge of the
water supply, of the foreman of the shop, and at times of the
public structure which the pipe served. The flat sheet was

---

[169] See Chap. I, section on Lead. Pliny (34, 161) says lead cost
about 1 cent a pound.

[170] Front., 116. It is assumed that the number in the groups
remained fairly constant.

[171] Gummerus (*P.-W.,* 1462) declares that there were two official
shops (see *C. I. L.,* VI, 4460 and 8461).

then bent, soldered, and equipped with the necessary bronze fittings. Four or five slaves could easily perform all of these simple operations.[172]

There are, moreover, two additional factors that have bearing on the question of the size of state production. Frontinus, by declaring that a good *curator aquarum* determined with care which proportion of the pipes were to be made by imperial slaves and which by private contractor (119), implied that state factories were not able to fulfil all the public needs. In fact, pipes leading from state buildings have been found which originated in the shop of private plumbers: a pipe from the fountain in the Forum Esquilinum (XV, 7303: 116-7 A. D.) bears the inscription *Annea Jucunda fecit*. Another private *conductrix* (7564) secured an imperial contract from the curator of the water supply in the first century; and there were two contractors, M. Plautus Eros and Sex. Egnatius Reditus, who made both public and private pipes.[173]   In the second place, the imperial freedmen whose names appear on pipes used by the state may have operated independent workshops, securing public contracts because of their former experience as slaves in the *familia aquarum*.[174]

Beneath the pavements of the city another network of pipes carried water from public aqueducts to private dwellings. To help identification in case of repairs or fraud the government required the maker to stamp the name of the owner of the household on the pipe, and frequently this *plumbiarius* added his own.   A study of the names of these workmen reveals the fact that few, if any, private pipes were produced in imperial workshops;[175] in the lead pipe industry, at least, there were no large government factories monopolizing pro-

---

[172] Lanciani, *I comentarii di Frontino intorno le acque e gli acquedotti*, 1880, 110 ff.; also Frank, *Econ. Hist.*, 241.

[173] For Eros see XV, 7523 and 25; for Reditus, 7333, 7409, 7512, and 7803.

[174] 7742: T. Flavius Tiridates; 7630-2: T. Flavius Hymnus; 7736, 7766, 7767: former public slaves at Ostia.

[175] The imperial freedman, Q. Athenaeus Aug. 1. (7799), may have had a private workshop.   To identify Ti. Cl. Felix on private pipes (7382, 7444) with Cl. Felix on imperial *fistulae* (7308-7309) is dangerous.

duction. The greater number of the makers of pipes for private use known from the stamps are freedmen with Greek
cognomina, though at times slave names appear and there is
evidence of plumbers (perhaps for repair work) among the
domestic slaves of the larger urban household. How many
slaves assisted individual shop owners is, of course, difficult to
determine; but since the name of the same maker rarely
recurs,[176] the assumption of large-scale production is unwarranted. There are even cases in which a large contract was
divided among several shops (XV, 7369-73).

Even among private plumbers, then, there is no evidence of
shops where large stocks of standardized pipes were accumulated. The need of recording the name of the individual
citizen to whose house the water was carried produced a system in which a new mould had to be made or an old one altered
to fit each name. The result was a simple method of manufacturing which demanded the concentration of a few trained
workmen.

From the materials considered in this chapter it appears that
the clearest example of an industry employing hundreds of
workmen was the making of bricks, though there is also slight
evidence for the large-scale production of clay lamps. Moreover, finds of both of these products in other lands indicate an
export trade, even if their bulkiness and the ease of production
prevented the creation of a large market. For these two
industries, Rome bore slight resemblance to Pompeii. Again,
in the making of bread, in tanning, and in fulling concentration into large shops was dictated by the need of machinery
and capital; so also in the production of fine furniture, of
glass, and of silver plate, the variety of skills demanded of the
artists resulted in manufactories of some size. Groups such
as these, however, existed at Pompeii, where the small artisan-
sales shop remained the essential method of production.

---

[176] A few exceptions may be noted: XV, 7370 and 7419 by Aurelius
Zosimus, 7487 and 7471 by Naevius Syntrophus, 7530 and 7573 by
Aurelius Florentinus. When the name of a woman takes the place
of the freedman *plumbiarius*, we are apparently dealing with an
entrepreneur who ran her several small shops with the aid of slave
foremen; on one pipe (7472) the foreman's name appears along
with that of the owner of the shop.

Furthermore, at Rome as at Pompeii no traces of factories have appeared from the excavations, and we search the sources and the inscriptions in vain for references to metal foundries or shoe factories. In the first place, there was no more labor-saving machinery available at the capital than at Pompeii and no more respect for the success that arose from business ventures.[177] Since, moreover, neither metal nor fuel was available nearby, Rome was not the natural location for large-size industries. Another decentralizing influence was the great number of rich households at the capital where skilled slaves catered to the needs of the wealthier part of the population. The demands that were not met in this way were often satisfied by finer articles produced by free labor in the provinces; for now that the seas were safe, commerce was prospering and Rome was the port to which all products came. To these contributing factors must be added the barriers set up by Roman law: since no patents offered protection to trade secrets, the factories that produced Arretine ware or Clodian silver did not hold together after the ware had been copied at other centres. The concentration of capital, probably the first necessity in manufacturing on a large scale, was also discouraged by the provisions of a code that required unlimited liability in the case of bankruptcy from all partners and forbade the foundations of corporations of limited liability in other than state business. These conditions necessarily resulted in the system of production described in the preceding pages.

---

[177] This contempt, a consequence of slave economy, reached its height at Rome, where slaves were most numerous and practically all business was in their hands or in those of Greek and Oriental freedmen (Gummerus, *P.-W.*, 1509; Kühn, *De opificum Romanorum condicione*, 1910, 36 ff.).

CHAPTER III

DISTRIBUTION

As shown in the preceding chapter the industry of the city was in the hands of craftsmen who, having fashioned copper kettles or gold rings in their small booths, sold them directly to a neighboring circle of patrons. Since, however, most of Rome's commodities were imported, in many of these small shops there was no work-bench, only a sales counter for clothing from the provinces or for the foodstuffs from far and nearby Italian fields. Between such petty retailers and the farmers of Campania or the shippers from Gaul there existed no machinery of distribution involving varied types of middlemen; at the arrival of a boatload of tunics from Patavium or of olives from Picenum the small merchants themselves flocked to the open-air markets by the river to purchase their stock in trade, and even the Tyrian and Palmyrene agents probably sold their costly stuffs directly from the warerooms. It is unusual for a wholesale dealer or a jobber to be mentioned in the sources or named in an inscription.

I. SHOPS, WAREHOUSES, AND MARKETS

Shops. For the retail merchants the sales facilities offered by the capital were unusual: the streets of ancient Rome as we can see them on such fragments of the Marble Plan as those numbered 179 and 37 were endless rows of galleries and arcades lined with shops. In addition, the state had provided public structures to aid in the distribution of the products necessary for the life of the imperial city. Many centuries before, the government, recognizing the ancient market day habit, had erected booths near the Forum for the use of small merchants; there the farmer who brought his fruits and vegetables to town could find clothing, trinkets, and tools to carry home.[1] Later the Basilica Aemilia and the Basilica

---

[1] The earliest shops built in the Forum are assigned to the first Tarquin (Livy, 1, 35, 10); they were state-owned and let out to

Julia, though built primarily to house the courts of law, on market days offered shelter to those engaged in such transactions. When toward the end of the republic traders were banished from the Forum, compensations were offered in varied forms: a portico along the Sacred Way, a basilica on the Clivus Argentarius, and a vast market hall on the Quirinal. By Hadrian's time the state had as many as five hundred shops to lease in the great *mercati* and *basilicae* throughout the city.

Horrea. Among the urban structures devoted to the needs of trade and commerce were spacious magazines and storerooms, over twenty of which are known to us by name.[2] Some lay in the Emporium district and received the goods coming by sea; others were constructed near the gates where important overland routes entered Rome; a few offered storage space and sales booths to merchants in the busiest centres of the city. In the thirteenth region near the Galban warehouse, the official depot for state grain and other produce,[3] were located other horrea designated as Seiana, Lolliana, Volusiana, and Petroniana. Cicero's friend, the edile M. Seius, had erected the magazine that bore his name probably for rental to private merchants,[4] and it is likely that the warehouse built by some member of the gens Lollia had also served this function before it became imperial property.[5]

---

dealers in foodstuffs, especially to butchers. Some time before 310 B. C., after the butchers had been moved to the Macellum north of the Forum, these booths were occupied by the *argentarii* (Platner-Ashby, 504; Viedebantt, "Forum Romanum," *P.-W.*, Suppl. IV, 463). Though trading took place every day, there was special activity on market days (see *Economic Survey*, I, 200-201).

[2] A full discussion of the location, function, and date of these horrea is given by Romanelli, "Horrea," *D. E.*, III, 967-90. See also Fiechter, "Horreum," *P.-W.*, VIII, 2458-64; Paribeni, *Optimus Princeps*, 1926, I, 170-1.

[3] See Chap. I, n. 6 for the Galbiana.

[4] Since Seius was noted for his distributions of oil and grain to the plebs at low rates in 74 B. C. (Pl., 15, 2; Cic., *de Off.*, 2, 58), the building of the warehouse probably reflects a bid for popular favor. The rooms lay southwest of the Galbiana, and in the early empire were let by a *conductor*, who was an imperial freedman (*C. I. L.*, VI, 9471). There is, thus, a suggestion of government ownership.

[5] In the first period the magazine belonged to the gens Lollia (VI, 9467); later to the family of Livia (VI, 4226, 4226a); and finally

No records attest the development of the private storerooms of the Volusii into an imperial warehouse,[6] but the Petroniana had come into the control of the state long before the Bithynian marble importer established his *statio* there.[7] This policy of letting space in government depots to private dealers is well established for the Horrea Galbiana and the famous bazaar on the Vicus Tuscus, the Horrea Agrippiana.[8] Unlike the storerooms by the docks this structure of Agrippa represents one of the earliest commercial structures available for small traders and petty shopkeepers in the centre of the city. Later, with the building of the warehouse of Nerva at the Porta S. Sebastiano between the Via Appia and the Via Ardeatina, rooms, booths, and storage space were rented to private dealers trading in the suburbs. The *lex* governing the terms of leasing the various sections of this warehouse has been preserved (VI, 33747), and its terms are probably applicable to other state magazines.[9] Additional

to the imperial house (about the time of Claudius: VI, 4239). See fragment 51 of the *Forma Urbis*.

[6] Romanelli (988) declares it was probably built by Q. Volusius Saturninus, who was consul in 56 A. D. The Volusii, rich landlords who invested so heavily in Italian wines and oils (see jars bearing their name in *C. I. L.*, XV, 4571, 4646, 4771, 4784), may have erected this depot to care for the products from their estates.

[7] M. Aurelius Xenonianus Aquila is mentioned in an inscription published in *L'année épigraphique*, 1926, no. 16. Aquila was either an imperial freedman or a native of Bithynia who had graciously adopted, as so many others had, the name of the Emperor Commodus after his world-wide bestowal of Roman citizenship. This warehouse had become state property under Nero (VI, 3971).

[8] For the Galbiana: *negotiator marmorum* (VI, 33886), *piscatrix* (VI, 9801), and *sagarii* (VI, 33906); for the Agrippiana: *vestiarii* (VI, 10026, 9972; XIV, 3958). See also *Röm. Mitt.*, XL (1925), 213-4, and XLI (1926), 229 for the organization of merchants (*negotiantes*) in the Agrippiana and the discussion in note 65 of this chapter. It has been generally assumed that these dealers rented the shops that surrounded the outside walls of the warehouse, but another theory has been advanced by Arvast Nordh, *Prolegomena till den Romerska Regionskatalogen*, diss. Göteborg, 1936. Since the locations in the Regionary Catalogues of the fourth century are not primarily the names of streets or temples, but of small districts (named from streets, buildings, fountains, and statues) used as convenient terms for administrative purposes, it is probable that the *opifex* inscriptions also give names of these sub-regions. Nordh has supported his thesis with sound evidence.

[9] See Romanelli (981-4), the commentary in Bruns (*Fontes Juris Romani*, 1909, 371), and *C. I. L.*, VI, 33860. The *conductor* leased

storage and sales rooms were provided by the horrea belonging to Q. Tineus Sacerdos near S. Martino ai Monti,[10] the
Horrea Ummidiana on the Aventine near S. Saba,[11] and
possibly by the Horrea Faeniana.[12] These buildings, however, are but a few of the public and private warehouses in the
city; the fourth century catalogue records a total of 290.[13]

Markets. Some of the wagons carrying fruits and vegetables from the farms outside the city went directly to the
houses of the wealthy; a greater number, however, stopped at
the municipal markets where the small dealers in foodstuffs
were gathered. As early as the third century B. C. the state
had provided open-air markets for special products by the
river, and after 179 B. C. a great central Macellum surrounded
by shops had been built north of the Forum.[14] As no mention
of this building occurs in the imperial period it had probably
been abandoned, but the Macellum Liviae was established
outside the Porta Esquilina to take its place. The open court
(80 x 20 m.) was surrounded by a hall of columns onto which

to the merchant warehouse space for the term of a year: the size
of these spaces varied from the *apothecae* through the *compendiaria*
and *armaria* to the *intercolumnia* and the *loca armaris*. The *horrearii* were freed from any liability in case fire or theft of merchandise, since the merchant was to assign his own *custos*.

[10] See VI, 33860 for terms of rental (Sacerdos was consul in 158
A. D.).

[11] The warehouse belonged to the Ummidii (M. Ummidius, consul
167 A. D.), who leased it to private merchants (the terms are on
an inscription published in *N. S.*, 1910, 90).

[12] The storeroom may have been built under the direction of L.
Faenius Rufus, prefect of the annona in 55 A. D. (see VI, 37796).

[13] At this time most of the horrea were safe deposit vaults where
citizens could store their valuables during the days of the military
anarchy (Romanelli, 971).

[14] Up to the year 210 B. C. there had been a Forum Boarium
(Cattle Market), Forum Holitorium (Vegetable Market), Forum
Piscatorium (Fish Market), and a Forum Cuppedinis (market for
fruits, honey, flowers). In 179 Fulvius Nobilior built a great market on the site of the Piscatorium, which had burned (see Schneider,
" Macellum," *P.-W.*, XIV¹, 129-133; Wymer, *Marktplatz-Anlagen der
Griechen u. Römer*, 1916, 22-23). Another fish market existed by
the Tiber near the spot where the best fish were caught (see Stöckle,
" Fischereigewerbe," *P.-W.*, Suppl. IV, 460). The square tufa building of great size recently excavated between the foot of the Capitoline
and the Tiber (see mention in *New York Times Magazine*, Feb. 14,
1937) was probably a market for the sale of produce that came up
the river.

many shops opened; remains show that not only dealers in comestibles but merchants of ointments, paints, and dyes were the occupants.[15] A little later, in 59 A. D., Nero erected on the Caelian the vast Macellum Magnum (Dio, 61, 18, 3). The two-storied portico which enclosed the rectangular court contained numerous shops, and a central building offered additional space to retailers.[16]

State interest in the city's food supply was shown not only by the establishment of these physical facilities but by a general supervision over fraudulent practices. A standard set of weights and measures was established,[17] under certain emperors market prices were regulated each year at the discretion of the Senate (Suet., *Tib.*, 34), and sumptuary measures in times of scarcity prevented the sale of costly and unusual dainties.[18] None of the sources mention the maintenance of sanitary conditions or the restraint of price-fixing combinations, but efforts along these lines must have been made.[19] As the control of the food supply passed gradually but steadily into the hands of the government, the work of the ediles, which had included the rental of the market booths and the collection of the market tax, was undertaken by a complex

---

[15] Schneider, 130 and Platner-Ashby, 322 (the dimensions given here are 80 x 25 m.). Fragment 60 of the *Forma Urbis* gives the general plan of this market, which continued to serve the city until the fourth century.

[16] An inscription of an *argentarius* located in this market during the early empire (*C. I. L.*, VI, 9183) is decorated with reliefs showing the sale of fish. The inscription, *cay da piscen, cay*, has been interpreted by Mommsen in the *Corpus* as *cedo, asses quinque; da piscem; cedo, asses quinque* (" give here, five asses; hand over the fish "). The reliefs and the inscription suggest retail dealing, but the presence of the *argentarius* needs to be explained. He may have been engaged in money changing in that part of the market devoted to the sale of fish; there may, however, be a hint of auctioneering activities and selling on a larger scale (see "Argentarius," *D. E.*, I, 659-60).

[17] The ancient table containing the standard measures used in the market at Pompeii has been found on the north side of the Forum (Mau, *Pompeii*, 88; Schneider, 133). For Ostia see *C. I. L.*, XIV, 376.

[18] Suet., *Jul.*, 43: watchmen were established in various parts of the market to seize delicacies exposed for sale in violation of the law.

[19] For anti-trust laws at Rome in the days of Plautus see *Captivi*, 489-495.

bureaucracy under the supervision of the *praefectus annonae*.
With the destruction of the historic Macellum north of the
Forum Romanum and the encroachment of the imperial fora
on the eastern part of the Subura the need for a market in
this section of the city had long been felt. The need was met
by the Mercato of Trajan, a vast hall of commercial character
which rose in a great facade beyond the eastern hemicycle of
the forum.[20] Here was assembled the most extensive series of
shops built by the state for commercial purposes. On the
ground floor of the three-storied exedra were eleven shops
which, unlike the open stalls in Nero's portico along the Sacra
Via, were separated from each other by a strong wall and
could be securely locked; these are of the usual size—3.1 m.
wide and 2.7 deep. On the first floor are eleven shops above
these on the outside of the hemicycle, and in addition one
small shop at each end at right angles to the hemicycle. Nine
of the eleven shops are approximately 3.90 m. x 7.1; the
others are smaller. Behind this outer row, facing on a dark
corridor, is an inner row of nine rooms, which in view of the
lack of light must have served as storerooms. The second
floor contains an outer row of nine shops (4.2 m. x 6.5) and
an inner row of five shops or *magazzini* at a higher level.
Shops have also been found in the attic story above the great
gallery, along the internal street called " Biberatica," and on
either side of the street which runs in a straight line from the
hemicycle to the Magnanapoli; along the lofty Aula Coperta
were twenty-four additional rooms; in the whole complex there
were about one hundred fifty booths. Entrance to these shops
could be gained not only by the two stairways leading up from
the ground floor of the forum but by streets leading into the

---

[20] A description of the Mercato is contained in the pamphlet issued
by Ricci, *Via dell'Impero*, 1933, 115-121; *id.*, *Il Mercato di Traiano*,
1929. Both these accounts have been brief and somewhat popular.
Boëthius and Riefstahl ("Appunti sul Mercato di Traiano," in *Roma*,
IX, n. 10e, 11-12 [1931]; X, n. 4 [1932]) have discussed relation-
ships with Oriental bazaars, with earlier Italian structures, and
with a scene on the Arch of Constantine. A complete bibliography
with some notes on new excavations has been published in *B.C.*,
LXI (1933), 253-257. See also Boëthius and Carlgren, " Die spätrepublikanischen Warenhäuser in Ferentino und Tivoli," *Acta Archaeologica*, III, 3, 1932, 181-208.

Mercato from the Subura, the Quirinal, etc.: there were in all five approaches to the building.

From the remains of the shops it seemed likely that various sections of the market were destined for the sale of special produce. The stores for the sale of grain, vegetables, and fruits were niches; other shops had small *piscinae* in the concrete floors where fish could be kept until sold; one of the booths in another group had a floor which sloped toward a small central hole. Ricci has suggested that the dealers of wine (or oil) placed small tubs here to receive the liquid that overflowed when wine was poured from a large cask into a purchaser's jar.[21] Other stalls were probably rented to retailers of fine imported cloth, furniture, plate, or even jewelry. In addition to these small units was a great covered gallery whose use can only be conjectured. Boëthius has compared the function of a hall of similar form in the great " warenhaus " at Ferentino to that of the Roman *atria auctionaria*,[22] and this Aula Coperta of the Roman market may very probably have served as one of the city's important auction centres.

It has been urged that the state erected this extensive market building merely to compensate the small dealers who had been removed from their independent shops by the imperial building programs, and the fact that the booths in the Mercato are of the standardized type developed from the small shophouse at Pompeii has been offered as additional evidence of their private character.[23] On the other hand, if the government had any interest in an organized system for disposing of the products coming to the fiscus and stored in imperial warehouses, evidence of that organization should certainly appear here. Consequently, when the references to

---

[21] *Via dell'Impero*, 117; also Lugli, " I Mercati Traianei " in *Dedalo*, X (1930), 527-51, especially 538. The holes in the floor, however, are found only in the dark storerooms and not in any of the rooms which could have served as shops. Lugli calls them the *magazzini* for the shops along the *Via Biberatica*.

[22] Boëthius and Carlgren, 186 and 206. These " warenhäuser " were not closed storerooms but a series of salesrooms open to the public. The floor of the great hall at Ferentino ascended gradually so that the upper platform, if used by an auctioneer, could be seen easily by the assembled salespeople.

[23] Boëthius, " The Neronian ' Nova Urbs,' " 90.

the *arcarii Caesaris* were first discovered, they were thought
to apply to imperial agents engaged in marketing or distributing state goods.[24] Now that these officials have been
shown to belong to the bankers' stalls in the forum and to have
had no connection with the Mercato, the most patent link
between the state and the market has been destroyed.[25] At
best, the evidence is slim, but some tribute in kind consisting
of grain or fruits, wool from imperial estates, papyrus and
linen from Egyptian state factories was constantly arriving
at the Horrea Galbiana,[26] and in no place could such wares
be distributed with greater ease, either directly through
imperial slaves or indirectly through small dealers, than in the
Mercato.

In addition to the three great municipal markets and the
open-air sales places by the river, certain districts in the city
became centres for the distribution of food products.[27] For
Martial the Subura was the marketplace which supplied him
with frost-bitten olives, waxy apples, cabbages, and Chian
figs (7, 31; 10, 94; see also Juv., 11, 136-41).[28] A second
commercial locality, the Velabrum, extended east of the Forum
Boarium: Horace mentioned it as " market centre " (*Serm.*,
2, 3, 229), and Martial praised the delicious cheese smoked
there (11, 52, 10; 13, 32). From the inscriptions we learn of
a wine merchant who had his shop in the Velabrum (*C. I. L.*,

---

[24] Lugli, 539. Finding in a Codex Vaticanus reference to the
arcarii Caesariani qui in Foro Traiani habent stationes, he suggested
that these officers of the fiscus not only received the wine, oil, and
grain coming to the state (which were temporarily stored in the
cellae vinariae, oleariae, etc., mentioned above) but supervised their
free distribution as *congiaria* and their sale at reduced prices to the
poor. The Aula Coperta served as the office and archives for the
directors. See also Boëthius' discussion in *Roma*, IX, n. 10 (1931).

[25] So Ricci, *Via dell'Impero*, 117; also *B. C.*, LXI (1933), 255.

[26] See Chap. I, n. 194.

[27] In the warehouse district near the Aventine a Porticus Fabaria
existed in the fourth century (*C. I. L.*, VI, 18; *Reg. Cat.* for Reg.
XIII). Moreover, if Hülsen's emendation of the Fasti of Ostia is
correct, dealers in vegetables gathered nearby, along the side of the
Circus Maximus next to the Aventine (see *Philologische Wochen-
schrift*, XL [1920], 307).

[28] Auctioneering activities in this district were carried on by M.
Livius M. l. Auctus (VI, 1953). Cf. also the *ferrarius de Subura*
(9399), the *lanarius* (9491), and the *lintearius* (9526).

VI, 9993) and of a dealer in wines and provisions at the nearby Fountain of the Four Scauri (9671). An *argentarius de Velabro* (money-changer·: 9184) supplements the evidence for commercial activities in this location.

II. MARKET PRODUCTS

Grain. Through the colonnades of the Horrea Galbiana passed a continuous stream of carts and porters conveying the sacks of Egyptian, African, and Campanian wheat from the Tiber barges to the storage rooms.[29] Still another train transferred over 12 million modii of it to the nearby Porticus Minucius, where it was distributed free to the poor.[30] Immediately the problem arises of the means employed by the government to dispose of the remaining nearly 50 million modii of tribute or state-purchased grain, for it is an acknowledged principle that the state regulated the sales price in order to keep it at a reasonably low level. To effect this result two methods of distribution were available: (1) to sell the grain directly to the populace from state horrea or (2) to deal through independent intermediaries, supervising the price and compensating them whenever undue circumstances caused fluctuations.

There is a statement in Horace (*Carm.,* 4, 12, 17-18) which seems, at first glance, to imply that the poet bought his cask of wine directly from the fiscal storeroom;[31] but since the evidence shows that there was no state-owned wine coming to the docks before the third century,[32] it is very probable that the dealer to whom Horace went was either a retailer who

---

[29] Representations of *saccarii* (*geruli, sarcinarii, baiuli*) at work have been preserved (Hug, "Saccarius," *P.-W.*, II², Zweite Reihe, 1620).

[30] From the time of Claudius this distribution had been made from the 45 sections of the porticus on various days of the month (see, for example, *C. I. L.*, VI, 10224: frumentum accepit die X ostio XXXIX). There were possibly two separate buildings: the *vetus* north of the Circus Flaminius and east of the Porticus Pompei and the *frumentaria* about 200 m. south (Hülsen, *B. C.*, LIV [1927], 94-100; Platner-Ashby, 425).

[31] Nardi parvus onyx eliciet cadum,
qui nunc Sulpiciis (= Galbianis) accubat horreis.

[32] See Chap. I, n. 14.

leased a shop in some corner of the warehouse or a merchant who kept his stock in a section rented to private traders. Waltzing, who believes in some direct trading by the state, supports his claim by using, in addition to numerous references from the third century, the account of Caesar's sale of African oil.[33] Neither of the sources which mention this tribute speaks of the sale, though in view of Caesar's desperate need of money it is probable. Like the requisition itself, however, the method of distribution would be unusual, for Caesar of necessity adopted the fastest and most lucrative means of distribution, probably selling directly from the ships. These two instances are scant evidence for direct selling on the part of the state in the early empire.

If the government disposed of its wheat directly from the warehouse, it is hard to explain the presence of entire guilds of *frumentarii,* for in view of the size of the annual Egyptian and African import the amount of trading on the open market would always be relatively small. In the time of Titus these retail grain merchants were numerous and wealthy enough to build a temple on property granted them by the state (*C. I. L.,* VI, 814).[35] Later, in the second century, the dealers in African grain and oil (VI, 1620) dedicated an honorary inscription to the prefect of the annona, probably in acknowledgment of special favors from the state in the form of increased facilities for securing grain from the storerooms or more agreeable regulations of the sales price. The existence of a Vicus Frumentarius in the Emporium district by the Aventine also implies concentration of the shops of such small merchants.[36]

---

[33] II, 23, n. 5 and 24.

[34] Plutarch, *Caes.,* 55 and Caesar, *Bell. Afr.,* 97. Both refer to an annual tribute of 3 million pounds of oil.

[35] They call themselves *negotiatores frumentari.* Although the term " negotiator " in the early empire often means wholesale trader and shipowner (see Cagnat, " Negotiator " in *D.-S.*), the smith Atimetus called himself a *negotiator ferrarius* (Chap. II, n. 99) and the retail grain dealer Megiste was a *negotiatrix.* See also *C. I. L.,* VI, 18 for the retailers engaged in *negotiatio fabaria.*

[36] In region XIII (*Reg. Cat.*; cf. also VI, 975). The *porticus annonarius* beneath the church of S. Maria in Cosmedin was probably the central administrative bureau of the annona and the residence of the prefect. Before 47 A. D. this hall had been usurped, with the tacit agreement of the authorities, by urban dealers, who controlled the arrival of the various merchandise from this advan-

One of these grain stores on the *scala mediana* (perhaps leading up the Aventine Hill) was owned by a *negotiatrix frumentaria et legumenaria,* Abudia M. l. Megiste (VI, 9683).[37] Granted that the whole policy of the state was non-interference with the retail dealer, it always kept a watchful eye on the sales price, knowing well that *inopia ac discordia* were concomitant. In particular it controlled the price at which the independent trader sold to the urban *frumentarius.* Suetonius tells us that in time of scarcity Augustus regulated the price of grain with no less regard for the interests of the farmers and the merchants than for those of the populace (*Aug.,* 42) ; but unfortunately he does not tell us of the method used. Again, when prices had reached a high level in the time of Tiberius, the dealers were paid two sesterces a modius to compensate them for selling at a lowered rate (Tac., *Ann.,* 2, 87) ; later, after the fire of 64, the emperor set the price of a modius at three sesterces (*Ann.,* 15, 39). In time of disaster, when price-fixing was necessary, such bonuses prevented independent traders from selling their cargo at other ports.[38] These occasions mentioned in the sources were undoubtedly the most important, but it is not unlikely that the state always regulated prices. Consequently, whether the retailer bought from the fiscal granary or from a ship newly arrived from Campania he paid the same price for a modius of wheat.[39]

Wine. The tremendous size of the wine import suggests a rather complex system of distribution, but the inscriptions of *vinarii,* though numerous, are not revealing. The skippers

---

tageously located site. The inscription *C. I. L.,* VI, 919 records its restoration to public use. See, however, the discussion of de Dominicis ("La 'Statio Annonae Urbis Romae,'" *B. C.,* LII [1925], 135-49), who sets aside this current identification.

[37] Grain dealers are named in the following inscriptions: VI, 9426, *frumentarius*; 9427, *frumentarius*; 9668, *negotiator frumentarius.*

[38] Even if these merchants carried but a few thousand modii of wheat any shortage in the city's food supply would be disastrous (Cicero, *de Domo,* 11; Tac., *Hist.,* 4, 38). Bonuses offered to merchants carrying African and Egyptian grain are discussed in Chap. I, nn. 21 and 22. See also Rostovtzeff, "Frumentum," *P.-W.,* VII, 143-4; Waltzing, II, 401 ff.

[39] As seen in the above citations, this averaged about 60 cents a bushel. Pliny (18, 90), however, gives the price of flour in his day as 40 asses (5 sesterces a modius), which means about $1 a bushel.

bringing the cargoes from Campania or Spain docked either at the warehouses at Ostia (*C. I. L.*, XIV, 430; 409) or at the *Forum Vinarium* (the *Portus Vinaria* is probably identical) near Monte Testaccio. The briskness of the trade at these docks and storerooms is suggested by the frequent mention of *coactores* (VI, 9181, 9189-90) and *argentarii* (VI, 9181-2) *de foro vinario*. The most important group is composed of the freedmen of P. Caucilius Callippus: they include a money-changer from the wine docks, the money-changer's freedman who follows the same profession, and a fellow freedman who calls himself a *coactor vinarius* (VI, 9181). Since the *coactor* was usually the middleman between the auctioneer and the buyer (the agent who collected the sums promised in large deals),[40] it is not unreasonable to suppose that the forum was the scene of important transactions in wine, possibly of auctions of incoming cargoes.

Among the traders here in the second century A. D. was a dealer in jars and bottles (*lagonarius*: VI, 37807). Inasmuch as the huge amphoras of Spanish wines were probably rebottled before being carried to the small shops of the city,[41] this C. Comisius Successus probably found a large market for his wares. Further details of the activities at the wine docks—the unloading, opening, and testing of the kegs—are available only for the third century when the sale of wine had become a function of the state:[42] but the *exasciatores* (cask openers), *haustores* (tasters), and *phalancarii* (porters) were undoubtedly at work in the forum during the earlier centuries.

By Trajan's day another wine magazine had been established on the right bank of the Tiber, the *cellae vinariae novae*

----

[40] See Von Premerstein, " Coactor," *P.-W.*, IV, 126; Mommsen, " Die pompeianischen Quittungstafeln," *Hermes*, XII (1877), 91-100.

[41] See Chap. I, n. 42.

[42] Cf. VI, 1785 (in the time of Aurelian) ; also Waltzing, II, 97-99. The casks were delivered to a district in the Campus Martius called *ad Ciconias Nixas*, and to each *possessor* (wholesale wine-dealer) 120 nummi were given for the transport of the cask to this spot. To the *exasciator* 10 nummi per cask were paid; the *haustor* received 30. The prices given to the watchmen and to the *phalancarii* are erased. For our period the prices have no value, but the list is important for defining various steps in the sales process. (For a discussion of the value, see Schwabacher, " Nummus," *P.-W.*, XVII², 1460.)

et Arruntianae (VI, 8826).[43] The dealers in this warehouse
had formed a guild, and a slave of Trajan (the one in charge
of the imperial larder, *dispensator*) had been granted immu-
nity from some magisterial duty in the group. It is possible
that this was a warehouse operated by the imperial slaves and
freedmen for selling the wine which came from the emper-
or's estates, but it is more likely that these horrea, like the
others, were let by the state to independent dealers. The term
negotiantes used by the guild-members seems to preclude the
assumption that the rooms were used to store wine destined for
palace uses.

A large number of the sherds of wine amphoras published
in *C. I. L.*, XV², were found not by the river but on the vigna
della Certosa in the agger near the Praetorian Camp.[44] The
consular dates on the inscriptions and indications of Campanian origin place them in the first century. At first glance
it would seem that the find represents either a large public
shop or a storeroom for wine destined for a neighboring market, but Dressel has shown that they were used simply as
refuse to fill in a hollow area. That the region of the Camp
was an important trading centre, however, is indicated by the
inscriptions of two wine dealers. One of these, who states that
he is a *vinarius in castris praetoriis* (VI, 9992) may have
been a large merchant who contracted to supply the needs of
the soldiers, though it is more likely that he had a large shop
in the sub-region which was named from the Camp.[45] The
business of Ulpius Eutyche(s), the imperial slave *negotians
cas(trorum) pr(aetorium)* (VI, 9661), can be defined with
no greater exactness. Furthermore, the one *conditarius*
(dealer in condiments) recorded for the city (VI, 9277) had
his shop in this district. The inscription is of interest because
of the fact that over twenty of the amphoras of garum recorded

---

[43] This rectangular structure had a series of vaulted storerooms
on the first floor and a complex of courts and halls on the second.
The first floor gallery was over 39 m. long, and rows of large stone
jars were found imbedded in the floor of the storage chambers (Olck,
" Cella," *P. W.*, III, 1876).
[44] See Dressel, *B. C.*, VII (1879), 36-64; 143-195, especially 193-5.
[45] See the conclusion of Arvast Nordh, n. 9 of this chapter.

in the *Corpus* have been found in the agger near the wine jars (*C. I. L.*, XV, 4687, 4694, 4706, etc.).

From the inscriptions of the remaining ten *vinarii* no additional details about methods of distribution can be obtained. The number, wealth, and obvious importance of the wholesale traders discussed in a previous chapter, however, indicate a correspondingly active retail trade.

Oil. In contrast to the numerous inscriptions of individual wine merchants the names of very few retailers of oil are known: L. Marius Phoebus, a dealer in Spanish oil from Baetica (VI, 1935); L. Cluvius L. l. Cerdo (9718), a retailer in the Carinae; L. Julius M. f. Volt. Fuscus, a merchant of oil from Gaul (9717); and C. Cerciens C. l. Dasius (9716).[46] This paucity of notices of large independent dealers may throw some light on the more usual type of oil vendor. According to the *Notitia* and *Curiosum* of a later century there were 2,300 places where oil was distributed to the population of Rome:[47] this means a petty merchant in every block, or even division of a block. It is not unlikely, moreover, that the later system of distribution reflects earlier conditions, for oil was one commodity that was needed in a hurry. Additional proof of the existence of large numbers of small dealers is found in two dedications made by organized groups of *oleari* to the prefect of the annona. In Hadrian's day the dealers in African grain and oil expressed their gratitude to the prefect (VI, 1620); in M. Aurelius' the traders in oil from Baetica honored him as their patron (VI, 1625b).

Meats. In the fourth century, when the government was distributing doles of meat to the inhabitants of Rome, the regulations controlling activities in the Forum Boarium, Forum Suarium, and Campus Pecuarius were formulated and set up on a marble tablet in the market places.[48] Even under

---

[46] The store of one of these dealers (a rather prosperous one) is probably pictured on a shop sign from the city which shows a booth covered with a linen awning. This awning protected the thirteen dolia stretched before the counter and the shopkeeper seated behind the counter recording sales in an account book (Jahn, pl. 13, 3).

[47] Richter, 389.

[48] VI, 1770-1 (363 A. D.). The regulations included careful weigh-

the organized regime of that period, however, direct dealing between the wholesale dealers employed by the government (*pequarii*) and the butchers (*lanii*) is implied. The only agents known from the inscriptions are the *actores de foro suario* of a guild of butchers in existence at the end of the second century (VI, 3728), but the usual meaning of the term " actor " implies aid in litigation rather than in financial deals.[49]

The merchants, several of whom are known by name,[50] probably brought their consignments of cattle to the open-air market by the river on Tiber barges; here the butchers purchased their stock and drove them off to the district around the Piscina Publica, where their abattoirs and retail booths were concentrated. The guild of butchers of the late republic (VI, 167: *Conlegiu Lanii Piscinenses*) had already centered their activities about this spot.[51] Naturally, however, small and large meat shops were scattered throughout the city: two are known from the Esquiline (VI, 33870; 37775, *ab Luco Lubentinae*) and one from the Viminal (9499).[52] The appearance of these stalls is shown on the funeral relief of Ti. Julius Vitalis and on the famous shop sign of the female dealer in geese,[53] though their large and varied stock probably

---

ing, the attribution of various parts of the animal to the *lanii*, and the terms of sale for the hides and flesh. See Waltzing, II, 90, n. 3 and 92, n. 6.

[49] The reliefs and the inscription on the famous Arch of the Money Lenders, on the other hand, indicate that important commercial enterprises of all types were carried on in this trading center (VI, 1035: 204 A. D.). The arch was erected to Severus and Caracalla by the bankers and the *negotiantes boari huius loci.*

[50] Q. Brutius P. f. Quir...., *mercator bov(arius)*, obviously a man of some position (VI, 37806); so also M. Antonius M. f. Claudia Teres, an importer from Misenum (VI, 33887). C. Julius Amarantus, *mercator de Foro Suario* (VI, 9631), probably belongs to the period after 200 A. D.

[51] By the end of the republic the butchers, who formerly had had their stalls along the Forum and in the Macellum, were grouped around the Piscina Publica of the twelfth region. See n. 1 of this chapter and Schneider, " Taberna," *P.-W.*, VIII, Zweite Reihe, 1866-7.

[52] In the third and fourth centuries the word *lanius* (butcher) is replaced by more definitive terms: *C. I. L.*, VI, 33900, *porcinarius* (dealer in pork); 31120, *pernarius* (dealer in ham); 1693, *suarii* (dealers in swine); 9278, *confectorarius* (dealer in dried pork).

[53] Jahn, pls. 13, 1 and 13, 2.

indicates greater prosperity than was enjoyed by the ordinary meat butcher.[54]

Flowers. By the fourth century A. D. there existed in Rome a Basilica Floscellaria for the retailing of flowers;[55] in the second century, however, the Portunium, a district near the temple of Portunus by the Tiber, was a recognized centre of the trade.[56] In view of the extensive use of garlands and festoons not only at private celebrations but in public festivals and for the decoration of shrines and temples,[57] the number of *coronarii* found in the city is not surprising, nor the early existence of a guild composed of rose vendors, violet sellers, and makers of wreaths (VI, 30707: late republic).[58] During the empire two groups of such dealers were organized with burial societies (VI, 4414 and 15). Although the wealthy possessed garland makers in their households (VI, 7009), the fastidious purchaser could find garlands to his liking either in the booths along the Sacred Way (9283), in the stock of M. Canius Zethus (9282), the *coronarius Vitellianus* (in the manner established by Vitellius), or in the candle and garland shop run by two imperial freedmen (9227).

III. CLOTHING

The more prosperous clothing stores in the capital were not unlike the establishment pictured on the Florentine reliefs: there were probably seats for the customers, clerks to exhibit the cloth, and a bargaining proprietor.[59] Although the thirty inscriptions of *vestiarii* at Rome usually record only the names of the shopowner and his wife (Greek freedmen for

---

[54] In addition, retailers of poultry (VI, 9674), of birds (9200), of fattened fowls (9201), and of ducks (9143) are recorded in the inscriptions.

[55] *Regionary Appendix*, Richter, 380.

[56] Fronto, *Ep.*, 1, 6, 14, with marginal notes (cf. Richter, 191): *in Portunio cum a coronariis veniunt.*

[57] Blümner, *Technologie*, I, 308-12.

[58] So Waltzing, IV, 14; see, however, " Coronarius " in *Thesaurus Linguae Latinae*, IV, 989.

[59] Amelung, *Führer durch die Antiken in Florenz*, 1897, nos. 167 and 168. Rostovtzeff (*Storia econ.*, facing 235) dates the reliefs in the first century A. D.

the most part), there are indications of two rather large groups. P. Avillius P. l. Menander (VI, 33920), whose shop was on the Cermalus, had three freedmen who either managed smaller branch shops for him or assisted him in his large store. Another group of clothiers, this time from an unknown location, *de Dianio* (33922) consisted of two freedmen and two freedwomen of a Cn. Munatius together with the freeborn husband of one of the *libertae*.

There is, moreover, evidence of considerable fortunes made in the sale of ready-to-wear clothing, a phenomenon rather unusual in Roman annals.[60] Suetonius (*de Gram.*, 23) enumerates the sources of income of that famous teacher of rhetoric, Q. Remmius Palaemon, who had started life as a slave in a weaving mill near Vicetia.[61] From teaching his income was 400,000 sesterces (about $20,000), but he doubled the amount by engaging in the wine trade and in the wholesale clothing business (*officinas promercalium vestium exerceret*). To distribute this ware, which he may have imported from the district where he had labored, Palaemon probably operated a chain of stores managed by his freedmen. It is quite possible that there were other wealthy clothing dealers like Palaemon: Seleucus the *centonarius* has already been mentioned,[62] and the model for Echion's master in all likelihood lived in Rome.[63]

The units of such interrelated shops, if operated by a single freedman, would undoubtedly be small. Additional evidence of their size is furnished by records of four tailors gathered at one street corner, the *Compitum Aliarium*.[64] In view of

---

[60] Though the business managers of Roman senators quietly lent the surplus to merchants, the risks were great in the absence of reasonable corporation laws and the profits were often small.

[61] Wessner, " Remmius," *P.-W.*, I, Zweite Reihe, 596-7. Pliny, who puts the date of his death in 76 A. D., also gives details of his investments in viticulture (14, 49).

[62] Chap. II, 75.

[63] Petronius, *Sat.*, 45. Echion was a *centonarius*, a slave of Titus. His master, who probably engaged in the clothing business, planned to give a fine gladiatorial exhibition for the town and according to Trimalchio *habet unde* ("he had the wherewithal").

[64] *C. I. L.*, VI, 9970, 9971, 4476, and *N. S.*, 1913, 70-1. Mancini, who published the last named inscription, suggests that this location may be one of the *vici* of the fifth region. Concentration of shops

the chance nature of such survivals, this proof of concentration is rather significant.

Several other districts in the city where small retailers of clothing gathered are designated in the inscriptions. First there are the Horrea Agrippiana. This storeroom, or more probably bazaar, situated south of the Forum between the Vicus Tuscus and the Clivus Victoriae, represents one of the earliest efforts (before 12 B. C.) on the part of the administration to increase the sales facilities of the capital.[65] Furthermore, the names of the clothiers, C. Julius Lucifer (VI, 9972) and M. Livius Hermeros (whose wife is Claudia Ti. f. Moschis: XIV, 3958), as well as certain peculiarities of orthography point to this early period. Although it is possible that these merchants had their booths in the sub-district named from the horrea, it is even more likely that they leased the booths which, as the Marble Plan plainly shows, surrounded its three inner courts. Since Lucifer is clearly an imperial freedman and Claudia's parents are apparently of the same origin, it may be that these *vestiarii* retailed the fine Egyptian linens or damasks which were being sent to Rome from the temple estates or as tribute from factories in Alexandria.[66]

---

on one street corner, however, is implied by the localities named *Decem Tabernae* (*Reg. Cat.*), *Tres Tabernae* (*ibid.*), etc.

[65] Fiechter ("Horreum," *P.-W.*, VIII, 2462) compares this bazaar to the Horrea Piperataria; Romanelli ("Horreum," *D. E.*, III, 987) believes it was a warehouse to let. The inscription found *in situ* speaks of a guild of *horreorum Agrippianorum negotiantes*, whose curators were Cn. Cossutius Eystrophus and L. Manlius Philadelphus. The three other members named are freedmen of Greek or Oriental extraction; none are imperial freedmen (Wickert in *Röm. Mitt.*, XL [1925], 213-14 and XLI [1926], 229). The three *cellae* of the horrea can be seen on fragments 37 and 86 of the *Forma Urbis*. Boëthius in his review of Shipley's *Agrippa's Building Activities in Rome* (*Wash. University Studies*, IV, 1933) calls attention to this early effort of the state to provide booths for private traders and compares the purpose of the building to the portico built by Nero along the Sacred Way (*Athenaeum*, XII [1934], N. S., 431-5). The *vestiarii de Cermalo Minusculo* (33920) also had their shop on that part of the Palatine near the Vicus Tuscus.

[66] Though there was no monopoly in the production of linen even in the third century, there was probably always some taxation in kind in Roman Egypt (see Persson, *Staat und Manufaktur im römischen Reiche*, 1923, 36-40; Warmington, *The Commerce between the Roman Empire and India*, 390). According to Statius (*Silvae*,

On the Vicus Tuscus, which passed along one side of the bazaar, were gathered dealers in fine clothing (*vestiarii tenuarii,* VI, 37826; *vestiarius tenuiarius,* VI, 33923; *vestiarius,* VI, 9976; *purpurarius,* XIV, 2433; and perhaps the *purpurari de vico* . . . , VI, 9848). It is interesting to notice that this epigraphical evidence is supported by Martial's statement that the best silk in Rome was to be found here (11, 27, 11). The largest of these groups (37826) is composed of three generations of freedmen of a L. Camerius: the *libertus,* L. Camerius L. l. Alexander, had a freedman, Thraso, who later became the patron of Cameria L. l. Iarine and apparently of her husband, Onesimus. Alexander's prosperity may have been the result of a special business connection with a fellow countryman who carried Coan silks or Eastern muslins on his merchant ship. On no other street in the city could such wares have been displayed more advantageously.[67]

On the other hand, dealers in workmen's blouses and rough cloaks for slaves apparently concentrated near the fiscal warehouse by the Tiber docks. Only one *sagarius* (VI, 33906) names his business locale as *de horreis Galbianis,* but three inscriptions (9864-66) have been found close by.[68] Although it is often impossible to determine whether places mentioned in inscriptions refer to actual buildings or to districts named from such buildings, some light may be thrown on the problem by the dedicatory inscription set up by the *curatores collegi(i) Herculis salutaris c(o)hortis I sagariorum* (VI, 339 and 30741). Romanelli, in an attempt to connect this inscription with the four mentioned above, proposes to identify the " first cohort " with one of the four spacial divisions of the Galban warehouse, a usage confirmed by many inscriptions.[69]

3, 3, 91) wool or cloth from the imperial estates at Tarentum came to the account of the fiscus. This wool could be stored in state warerooms and sold in state shops.

[67] Dealers in pepper and perfumes were also gathered here (Porphyrio on Hor., *Ep.,* 1, 20, 1; 2, 1, 269-70).

[68] Romanelli, 979-80.

[69] VI, 588, 30901, etc. This use of the term "cohors" does not exclude a quasi-military organization of the warehouse workers, which had been previously set forth by Dessau, Hirschfeld, and Gatti.

According to his interpretation, the dealers had sales booths, or storerooms, within the horrea (in the first court), either before or after it had become state property.[70] If, as seems likely, much of the merchandise was imported from Gaul, convenient depots near the harbor would be desirable; at those stalls small retail shopkeepers in distant parts of the city could purchase their stock.

A second important trading centre for the *sagarii* were the famous shops that surrounded the Theatre of Marcellus.[71] In Trajan's day the dealers from this building and the surrounding district had formed a guild (VI, 956: 104 A. D.) which was rich enough to dedicate a marble monument to the emperor. Possibly, the dedication expressed gratitude for the awarding of a contract to supply the *vigiles* or the cohorts at Ostia;[72] probably, some arrangement in the terms of the rental for the theatre shops had occasioned the monument. Other state shops in the great arcade which surrounded the Circus Maximus were, in all likelihood, rented to clothiers.[73]

Unlike the inscriptions of the *vestiarii*, which in general name a single dealer, those of the *sagarii* record large groups, and among these groups several *nomina* appear with remarkable frequency. For example, five freedmen of a L. Salvius, four of whom have Celtic *cognomina*, were engaged in importing and distributing such woolens from the mills around

---

[70] Another interpretation would separate the word *sagariorum* from the preceding words and have the guild of dealers in blouses make a dedication to Hercules, the patron god of the workers of the first division of the horrea. Yet even this explanation implies a close connection between the warehouse shops and the merchants of the *sagum*.

[71] Three series of open arcades, suitable for shops, surrounded the outside of this theatre situated near the Tiber and the Vegetable Market. For recent excavations see Pernier, "Studi sul teatro di Marcello," *B. C.*, LV (1928), 5-40 (plate I shows the booths still in use during the sixteenth century).

[72] Not only were *saga* used for blankets and saddle cloths, but formed the ordinary costume of the common soldier (Fiebiger, "Sagum," *P.-W.*, II, Zweite Reihe, 1753-5). Supplies for the armies in the provinces were, of course, produced on the spot.

[73] According to Tacitus (*Ann.*, 15, 38) the great fire of 64 started in the shops *quibus id inerat mercimonium quo flamma alitur*. Dionysius of Halicarnassus (3, 68) describes the innumerable workshops in the arcade that surrounded the Circus.

Padua.[74] For the *sagarii* who were freedmen of Q. Cornelius, however, the names offer no evidence for determining the nature of their work. The most likely assumption is that Quintus owned a chain of shops operated by his freedmen Antipho (VI, 9866), Nicephor (9867), Philomusus (9868), and Menippus (9869); in fact, the location of Philomusus' shop *a theatro Marcelli* is defined in the inscription. An even more extensive group of shops is implied by the names of seventeen freedmen (and two slaves) found on the tombstone of the *sagarius*, A. Caecilius Spendo (9865). Although there is no proof that all the former slaves were engaged in the same occupation as their patron, it is quite probable that they were. From the slight information available for the clothing industry at Rome, moreover, we may conclude that the Caecilii did not work as a group in one store but as managers of small units.

IV. JEWELRY AND METAL WORK

Rome's position as centre of the jewelry industry resulted not only from the demands of a rich city and a luxurious court but also from fiscal ownership of the chief gold mines and from the arrival of numerous ships from Alexandria bringing pearls and other gems from the Far East. Dealers in these pearls are named with unusual frequency in the inscriptions of the city.[75] For them the Sacred Way had been the main place of distribution since the last years of the republic: of the twenty-two known inscriptions of artisans and retailers whose shops were in this region,[76] eighteen are of jewelers or dealers in precious stones. In the early days the censors had supervised the erection of a row of small shops

---

[74] See Chap. I, n. 116.
[75] There are about seventeen inscriptions of *margaritarii*. According to Pliny (9, 106; 37, 204) pearls were in greater demand than any other jewel. See Rommel, "Margaritai," *P.-W.*, XIV², 1695-6.
[76] Two of *aurifices* (*C. I. L.*, VI, 9207; *Eph. Ep.*, IX [1913], 438); two of *caelatores* (VI, 9239; 9221); two of *flaturarii* (9418, 9419a); one of a *vascularius* (37824); one of an *auri aceptor* (9212); one of a *auri vestrix* (9214); one of a *coronarius* (9283); one of a *tibiarius* (9935); one of a *unguentarius* (1974); one of a *pigmentarius* (9795); two of *gemmarii* (9434-5); and seven of *margaritarii* (9545-9; 33872; X, 6492).

on either side of the street, and after the Augustan rebuilding program they were surmounted, on the north side at least, by a structure resembling the bazaar of the later horrea.[77] It was Nero, however, who, in his reconstruction of this section of the city in 64 A. D., offered to the dealers in luxury an elaborate system of from 150 to 200 new shops.

Nero's lofty arcade with the spacious portico behind it was of a type commonly found in southern European cities: it was intended primarily for enjoyable strolling but merchants were allowed to expose their wares in the space between successive columns (on the north, 5.3-5.4 m. wide; on the south, 4.4-4.5 m.). Traces of separating walls do not appear before the third century, and unless the sections were enclosed in grills, of which no evidence has survived, it would have been necessary for the dealers to bring their precious wares to the portico each morning and to take them away again at night. Since the whole length of the arcade on either side of the street was under one roof,[78] the portico apparently marks a step toward the large variety store; it must be remembered, however, that the separate parts of the " store " remained independent shops.[79]

Although with a single exception these merchants bear Greek cognomina and are obviously of servile origin, there is abundant evidence of their material success. L. Calpurnius

---

[77] For a discussion of these shops see Van Deman, " The Sacra Via of Nero," *Memoirs of the American Academy in Rome*, V (1925), 115-126 and " The Neronian Sacra Via," *A.J.A.*, XXVII (1923), 383-424.

[78] The arcade, reached by a flight of steps from the street, extended on the north from the temple of Antoninus and Faustina to the Clivus Palatinus and on the south from the Regia to the same street. On the south side were over thirty piers, and a smaller number on the north (" The Neronian Sacra Via," 124).

[79] Of the seven *margaritarii* from this street, two at least can be dated from letter forms and orthography before the building of the Neronian structure: VI, 9545 and X, 6492; the others belong to the first half of the first century A. D. (see Gummerus, " Die röm. Ind.," 273). Their concentration in this district during the early empire has been further substantiated by the finding of one of their shop signs (VI, 37804) near the Temple of the Deified Romulus (published in *Röm. Mitt.*, XX [1905], 115-117). Four additional pearl dealers are known who apparently were not in this district, but only one names the location of his shop—the Velabrum (VI, 37803).

L. l. Antiochus Nicaeus Maior (who shows by his second cognomen that he had been born in Asia Minor (VI, 33872) after winning his freedom, or perhaps even before, had established his jewelry business near the Sacred Street. His son, proudly styling himself L. Calpurnius Antiochus, the son of Nicaeus, of the tribe Cornelia, also became a *margaritarius de sacra via* and was so successful in his chosen profession that he acquired a freedwoman and probably two freedmen (VI, 9546). Further evidence of the lucrative nature of traffic in pearls is shown by the inscription of Tuticius Hylas (1925: end of the second century). Hylas, honorary president of the guild of the *dendrophoroi,* bequeathed to his fellow members the sum of 10,000 sesterces (about $500), the interest from which was to be used each year for a memorial service in his behalf. Another pearl merchant, M'. Poblicius Hilarus, also became a leading spirit in the same group in the time of the Antonines (30975). A large portrait statue of him was erected in the vestibule of the basilica where the guild held its meetings, and we can be sure this honor resulted from some unusual beneficence.[80]

Like the goldsmiths and silversmiths known from the inscriptions, some of these *margaritarii* undoubtedly combined the functions of artists and salesmen, boring the pearls and encasing them in settings. To aid these craftsmen in securing a market for their wares, the state provided a trading centre adjoining the Forum of Caesar, the Basilica Argentaria. An inscription from Veii (*C. I. L.,* XI, 3821, *de basilica vascularia aurarius et argentarius*), dated by its letter forms to the early empire, is generally interpreted as referring to this building.[81] If this attribution is correct, it argues against the statement that the building was primarily the official location of the public bankers who, driven from the Forum by the expanding affairs of state, exercised their calling in this hall with its

---

[80] The *schola,* generally known as the Basilica Hilariana, was excavated in the vigna Casali on the Caelian hill (*B. C.,* XVIII [1890], 18-26).
[81] Gummerus, "Die röm. Ind.," 291. A Basilica Argentaria is mentioned in the *Regionary Catalogue* for the eighth region, and a Basilica Vascularia, possibly the same building, is named in the *Appendix.*

adjacent booths along the Clivus Argentarius.[82]   From the excavated shops and Basilica it has been determined that work was begun under Domitian, or even Vespasian, and completed by Hadrian; the *graffiti* preserved on several of the pillars, however, belong to the time of Trajan.   Some scratchings of a commercial nature have been preserved, but unfortunately none have reference to the sale of silver plate.[83]

In this same Hall of the Silversmiths the pots, buckets, and fibulae from Capua in all likelihood were retailed.[84] The *sodales aerari a pulvinar(e)* (VI, 9136), however, sold their wares near the loge where the emperor viewed the circus games.   Since one of the members of the group was an imperial slave, it is possible that through his former connections with the court he had secured this advantageous sales place.   The location of the shop of L. Lepidius L. l. Hermes, *negotiator aerarius et ferrarius sub aede Fortunae ad Lacum Aretis* has not been determined.

V. LUXURY WARES

The Campus Martius.   In addition to the fashionable shopping district in Nero's portico and along the Clivus Argentarius, there was another centre where " golden Rome flings about its wealth " in the Campus Martius around the Saepta Julia and the Porticus Argonautarum (Mart., 10, 80, 4; Stat., *Silvae*, 4, 6, 2).   The portico (about 60 x 400 m.) surrounding the voting precinct had been completed and decorated by Agrippa during that period when Augustus with the aid of his friends was attempting to make the Campus one of the beauty spots of Rome.   The shops in it, clearly visible on fragments 34-6 of the Marble Plan, are brought to life

---

[82] Ricci, *Via dell'Impero*, 40, and for a description of the excavations, 38-44.   Both Platner-Ashby (76) and Boëthius (*Die Antike,* XI [1935], 122-4) declare it was a hall reserved for silversmiths. See also Van Buren, *Ancient Rome*, 100-104.

[83] Discussed by Della Corte, " Le Iscrizioni Graffite della ' Basilica degli Argentari ' sul Foro di Giulio Cesare," *B. C.*, LXI (1933), 111-130.   No. 79 records the buying of a slave and no. 80 the itemized account of personal debts.   Money-lenders would doubtless have stalls in this exchange centre.   Here too we may probably place the *negotiatores vascularii* (VI, 1065: time of Antoninus Pius).

[84] See Chap. I, n. 157.

by Martial's detailed account of the disastrous shopping trip of Mamurra (9, 59). In the interior of the first shop young slaves were offered for sale; in the next, table tops of rare woods with glistening ivory legs, and tortoise shell couches large enough for six. From here Mamurra passed to the booths where Corinthian bronzes, statuary by Polycleitus, and antique tankards were displayed. Nearby in the jeweler's shop sardonyx, jaspers, myrrhine vessels, and tinkling pearl earrings were exposed for his inspection. And finally, there was the stall where Mamurra could buy his penny cups. Juvenal's description of a more profitable trip (6, 153-5) has as its setting a corresponding series of booths about the neighboring Porticus Argonautarum. The shopper was not content with the cheap clay figures put on sale for the festival of the Sigillaria; she insisted on seeing the real stock behind the improvised canvas flaps, and carried home a vase of crystal, a myrrhine vessel, and a diamond.[85] Similar booths must have surrounded the numerous porticoes of this district.

The Horrea Piperataria. The size of the trade in spices, ointments, and perfumes is suggested by about thirty inscriptions of urban *unguentarii* and *thurarii,* and the existence of a warehouse devoted to the reception and distribution of such Eastern products (the Horrea Piperataria) is proof of an enormous import. Of the three state depots for special products at Rome (the Chartaria, Candelaria, and Piperataria)[86] this structure alone can be dated with certainty before the period of Aurelian; furthermore, the time and purpose of its establishment has some bearing on the imperial policy toward trade.

Though one ancient source, and that of little value, assigns the completion of the spice market to Domitian in 91 A. D.,[87] archaeological evidence points to the building era

[85] See scholium *ad loc.:* . . . tempore Saturnaliorum sigillaria sunt. Tunc mercatores casas de linteis faciunt [quibus picturam (the mural) abstrudunt].

[86] For the Chartaria see below, n. 108. The Candelaria is known only from frag. 53 of the Marble Plan (the time of the Severi). Romanelli ("Horrea," *D. E.,* III, 969) has suggested that this was a fiscal storeroom for the wax tribute mentioned in Pliny, 21, 77.

[87] Chronograph of the year 354 A. D. (ed. Mommsen, *Monumenta*

following the death of Nero. It has been suggested that it was Vespasian who recalled the pleasure portico along the Sacred Way to mercantile uses.[88] There are, moreover, additional factors which attest Vespasian's interest in enlarging state revenues by commercial projects.

Consideration must be given first of all to the emperor's statement (recorded in Suet., *Vesp.*, 16) that he needed two billion dollars (forty billion sesterces) to set the business of government in order. We also know that because he overlooked no possible source of income nicknames of "The Muleteer" and "The Salt Fish Dealer" were contemptuously flung at his head.[89] According to Suetonius, moreover, he was so interested in the income from trade that at times he would buy up certain commodities merely to distribute them at a profit, and it is likely that such transactions were not directed toward personal but toward fiscal advantages. In his constant attempt to increase and readjust state finances, Vespasian's attention must have been directed to the drain of imperial currency to the East, for a member of his cabinet, Pliny the elder, knew that one hundred million sesterces ($5,000,000) were sent annually to India, China, and the Seres (Pl., 12, 84). He also knew that fifty-five million ($2,750,000) of this amount were absorbed by India, mainly for spices, ointments, and gems (6, 101). Pliny's frequently stated concern about this adverse balance probably reflected the emperor's attitude. That Vespasian began at once to apply remedial measures is indicated not only by the cessation of complaints about the drainage of the empire's wealth but by

---

Germaniae Historica, I, 1892, 146). Dio (72, 24) records the destruction of a warehouse in this location in the fire during Caracalla's reign.

[88] Van Deman, "The Neronian Sacra Via," 425. The slight contradiction in dating may only mean that the completion of the horrea was delayed for a period of years. Domitian, as the chronographer states, probably dedicated the market.

[89] Dio, 65, 8 (cf. Suet., *Vesp.*, 19). His father had been an auctioneer's assistant and the future emperor himself, after an honest governorship in Africa, had been so poor he had been forced to trade in mules. Here was no aristocrat unacquainted with the value of money. See also Charlesworth in *The Cambridge Ancient History*, XI, 1936, 2 ff.

the decrease in the coin hoards of India after his reign.[90] The need for money, the interest in Indian trade, and the establishment of a spice warehouse at this time suggest a problem.

The place at which Vespasian could interfere with the Eastern traffic in spices was the province of Egypt. Plant products from India, landed at Myos Hormos and conveyed by caravans from the Red Sea, came to the entrepôt of Alexandria for shipment to the ports of the empire.[91] Many of these spices undoubtedly arrived at Alexandria in a raw state and were prepared for distribution in the factories existing there; of one of these, that in which frankincense was purified, Pliny has left a brief but vivid picture (Pl., 12, 32). There is, of course, little reason to believe that the Romans had continued the Ptolemaic monopoly in this branch of industry, but there are numerous other ways in which some part of the output of these factories could come into the imperial fiscus.[92] If Vespasian inaugurated a change in policy toward such factories, a possibility discussed below, he might replace the silver and gold coinage going toward India by their output. The result would be the decrease in coin finds already mentioned.[93]

The theory of imperial interest in the Egyptian perfume factories is supported by the extant clay seals from Alexandria with the legend " the spices of Caesar." [94] Varied explanations of their use have been offered,[95] but almost all concede

---

[90] Warmington, 88-89 and 293-4.

[91] Warmington, 7. The high tariff (25 per cent) exacted at Arabian ports (*Periplus*, 19) would also tend to throw the commerce through Egypt.

[92] By the third century taxes in kind (the *anabolica*) were shipped each year from Alexandria to the *horrea fiscalia* (S. H. A., *Aur.*, 45). Aurelian probably only regularized existing requisitions. Taxes of this type could be exacted from state-owned factories, farmed out to lessees, or from privately owned units (see Persson, 25-29).

[93] Since there is no evidence for a corresponding decline in commerce with the East, Warmington has suggested (293-4) that barter in the products from the provinces—especially from the factories of Egypt—was replacing transactions in metal.

[94] Heichelheim, " Monopole," *P.-W.*, XVI[1], 194-5.

[95] Heichelheim (*ibid.*) intimates they represent taxes in kind, as does Warmington, 304-5, nn. 90-1. Schmidt (*Drogen und Drogenhandel*, 90) declares that these products from Alexandrian shops were sent to Rome for the use of the imperial palace, and were

that they represent some form of tribute in kind. At this point it may be well to notice the inauguration by Vespasian of the Fiscus Alexandrinus, with its headquarters at Rome. The purpose of the chest has been differently interpreted, but it has generally been explained as the bureau to which were sent the proceeds of the poll-tax instituted by Vespasian.[96] There is no doubt, however, that the new emperor was interested not only in money but in confiscated properties. Dio, in explaining the peculiar hatred the Alexandrians bore him for his revival of obsolete taxes and his establishment of new exactions, declares that they were particularly displeased because he had confiscated the greater part of the royal properties (65, 8). The new fiscus probably received the revenues from these confiscations. Moreover, these regal estates undoubtedly included houses, factories, and industrial quarters: some may have continued to be operated as imperial property; others may have been let out to private producers. From both sources manufactured goods could be sent to the fiscus at Rome, for in view of the peculiar relationship in which Egypt stood to the Roman state and the person of the emperor, it is likely that the principle of tribute in kind had always been operative here.

Be that as it may, a spice market was built in Rome at this period on the Sacred Way, and a little later a new road, the Via Domitia, took care of the traffic between this urban district and Puteoli.[97] The construction of a market and a

---

therefore tax-exempt. Rostovtzeff (*Röm. Mitt.*, XIII [1898], 121-3) states that these shipments came from India tax-free, carried on ships that had been sent out by the government in connection with state manufactories at Alexandria. Unfortunately, the date of the seals is not known; they may even be part of the *anabolica*.

[96] Hirschfeld (*Verwaltungs.*, 371 ff.) connects the chest with the tribute grain sent from Egypt; Johnson (*Roman Egypt*, 494) declares the function of this fiscus is unknown; Rostovtzeff ("Fiscus," *P.-W.*, VI, 2402-3 and "Fiscus," *D. E.*, III, 125-6) believes that the chest was established by Vespasian to receive the poll-tax exacted from the Alexandrians but adds that all Alexandrian taxes and tribute were included in it. The metal tags found at Rome marked "Fiscus Alexandrinus" seem to prove that the shipments included more than money.

[97] The construction of the road suggests an increase in the number of vessels which usually docked at Puteoli (Warmington, 90).

road may merely indicate that with the increase of private trade Rome had gradually usurped the place of Capua as distributing centre of the western perfume trade. There is, however, another bit of evidence in Pliny which does point to some form of state interest in the market—if only a close supervision and control of prices. In his twelfth book he gives a long list of the cost of spices and perfumes in his day, distinguishing the numerous varieties (as in pepper) and assigning to each a price.[98] Not only does this detailed list raise speculations as to its source, but the surprisingly small number of prices that show variation hints at regulation. It is not improbable that Pliny collected his information from the stalls in the newly organized horrea.

The evidence, incomplete as it is, suggests that the state under Vespasian's direction had more interests involved in a new spice market than the revenues to be gained from the rental of private stalls. The need for money at the beginning of Vespasian's reign, his interest in the adverse trade balance, his previous experience in commercial enterprises, the emergence of a Fiscus Alexandrinus, and perhaps even " the spices of Caesar " may all be connected with the Horrea Piperataria.

Knowledge of the state's method of disposing of products sent to the market is lacking, but Pliny's description of the transactions involved in the balsam trade intimates that in his time an intermediary operated between the fiscus and the consumer.[99] And yet by the time of Galen, whose residence in Rome extended intermittently through the reigns of Marcus Aurelius and Commodus, imperial procurators shipped rare drugs and spices from all parts of the empire directly to the horrea,[100] and it is not unlikely that these were sold directly to small retailers or to individuals.

---

[98] The prices are collected and discussed by Schmidt, 104-106.

[99] Pliny, 12, 111-123. The royal balsam gardens of Judea became an actual monopoly of the fiscus after Titus' conquest. With regard to the wholesale and retail prices Pliny writes: quippe milibus denarium sextarii empti, vendente fisco tricenis denariis veneunt ("for a sextarius of balsam, which is sold by fiscal authorities at 300 denarii [$60], is sold again for a thousand [$200]").

[100] See Chap. I, 53. Of course, many of the drugs the court physician mentions were sent directly for the use of the imperial household.

Independent Dealers in Perfumes and Ointments. Famous among these dealers at the end of the first century were Martial's Cosmos, the perfumer mentioned in fifteen epigrams, and Niceros, the city's chief cinnamon dealer. Because of the special breath pastilles and hair ointments that bore his name, however, Cosmos was probably not only a merchant but a manufacturer on a rather large scale.[101] It is significant that he had his shop at Rome; perhaps the recent erection of the horrea had influenced the establishment and the size of his business.

Earlier, in the last days of the republic, an *unguentarius* (M'. Poblicius Nicanor: *C. I. L.*, VI, 1974) had a shop on the Sacred Street, at the time when the neighboring Vicus Tuscus served as the center for dealers in *tus et odores et piper et quidquid chartis amicitur ineptis* (Hor., *Ep.*, 2, 1, 269-70).[102] Since Capua, through the reign of Nero at least, continued to be the centre of the production of perfume in Italy (Pl., 21, 16-17) most of the *thurarii, unguentarii,* and *aromatarii* assembled on these two streets were obviously distributors. That their trade was of long standing is shown by a dedication made to Jupiter Optimus Maximus by the guild of *aromatarii* in the reign of Augustus (VI, 384; this is, moreover, the 28th *lustrum* of the organized perfumers). The social status of the members may be inferred from the fact that the president was a freeborn Roman, T. Annius T. f. Col. Philippus. The subsequent history of the group, however, is unknown, for neither the guild nor the term *aromatarius* appears in urban imperial inscriptions.

Among the spicers and perfumers of the early empire the names of Popillius and Cornelius recur with unusual frequency (*C. I. L.,* VI, 845, C. Popillius Primio; 10003, C. Popilius [*sic*] C. l. Phileros; 10001, C. Popillius Anthus;

---

[101] Specialties that bore his name were pastilles (1, 87, 2), spices containing cinnamon (14, 146, 1; 3, 55, 1), and a special woman's perfume (14, 59, 2). Stein ("Kosmos," no. 2, *P.-W.*, X, 1499) discusses his activities. For Niceros see Martial, 6, 55, 3; 10, 38, 8; 12, 65, 4.

[102] In the fourth century the Vicus Tuscus was called the Vicus Turarius (Porphyrio, *ad loc.* and *ad* Hor., *Ep.*, 1, 20, 1).

see also 9931, P. Cornelius P. l. Eros, and 9930, P. Cornelius P. l. Antiochus). If these freedmen represent *institores* of a rich Popillius or Cornelius (the only *institor* named in the urban inscriptions is Faustus Po . . . *institor unguentarius,* VI, 10007,),[103] an extensive chain of shops must be assumed. A similar group of shops was probably operated in the days of the republic by the freedmen of the *thurarii,* Gaius and Publius Trebonius (VI, 9993) : on their tomb eleven freedmen and freedwomen (all with Greek or Oriental cognomina) are specified as "freedmen and perfumers." Perhaps the house of the Trebonii may be compared to the famous Faenii, who were large-scale distributors of perfumes at Capua, although there is no indication that the Roman concern employed agents in other cities.[104] The Faenii as well as the Trebonii, however, probably supplied the capital for a Greek or Egyptian shipper who made a yearly trip to the spice-bearing lands east of the Red Sea.

A hint of the vast profits to be made in the retailing of ointments, aromatics, and pepper is given by the size of the marble tablet dedicated by C. Popillius Primio to Nero (VI, 845). This dealer's gratitude may have had some connection with governmental interference in checking the price-raising tricks of the customs-collector, Demetrius (Pl., 33, 164) who, it will be remembered, had been demanding import duties in excess of the amounts for which he had contracted. The *tota Seplasia* (perhaps the district at Rome as well as at Capua) had brought the publican to trial before the consuls.[105]

VI. THE BOOK TRADE

The importance of papyrus in the life of the city is forced to the attention by Pliny's account of the paper crisis in the

[103] Dessau, *Inscriptiones Latinae Selectae,* 7608 completes it Po(pili?). See the section on *Institores* below.
[104] At Rome there are records of L. Faenius Telesphorus, *unguentarius Lugdunensis* (VI, 9998), who operated in Gaul, and also of L. Faenius Primus (5680) and L. Faenius L. ɔ. l. Favor, importers of Capuan wares to the capital (9932). L. Faenius L. l. Alexander was at Puteoli (X, 1962), and L. Faenius Ursio at Ischia (X, 6802).
[105] As a result of such extortions Nero established a firmer control over the tax collectors (Tac., *Ann.,* 13, 51). See Philipp, "Seplasia," *P.-W.,* IV, Zweite Reihe, 1546; and Schmidt, 80.

reign of Tiberius (13, 89): as a result of the complete dis-
arrangement of the ordinary relations of life, he tells us,
members of the senate were appointed to regulate the distribution of the Egyptian import. Such regulation by a senatorial commission combined with Pliny's account of Fannius'
papyrus factory [106] makes it clear that for the first century,
at least, there was no government monopoly in the distribution
of papyrus. This conclusion is supported by records of the
private production and sale of papyrus in Egypt.[107]

In the third century, on the other hand, there was in existence at Rome a Horrea Chartaria, from which the government
sold the paper sent as annual tribute from Egypt.[108] Since
it is not likely that this state interest was of sudden appearance, some tribute in kind during the earlier centuries may
be assumed.[109] Moreover, the assignment of a Roman soldier
to the Fayûm *ad chartam conficiendam* in the reign of
Domitian suggests government control of production in these
important marshes; [110] for this region, it will be noted,
with the accession of Vespasian had passed from the category
of imperial *res privata* to that of public property. Perhaps
in paper production in the Fayûm as in the perfume and
spice industry, this emperor had found a new source of income
for the state. Furthermore, the amount of usiac land in
Egypt must always have forced the Roman emperor to
act to some degree at least as head of a large industrial
undertaking.[111]

---

[106] Discussed in Chap. II, 100-1.
[107] Johnson, 328-30; 359-61; Lewis, *L'Industrie du papyrus dans
l'Égypte gréco-romaine*, 1928, 133-135.
[108] In region IV: on the Esquiline near the temple of Tellus (*Not.
Reg.*). Romanelli (968) connects the crisis with Suetonius' statement of Tiberius' interest in revenues and monopolies (*Tib.*, 30)
and with the establishment of the horrea. This interpretation, however, strains the meaning of the term "monopolium." Lewis (140)
puts the erection of the warehouse in the time of the Severi or the
late Antonines, when the return of natural economy had revived the
principle of taxes in kind.
[109] Rostovtzeff, *Storia econ.*, 503-4, n. 57; Lewis, 140, n. 2.
[110] Johnson, no. 407, p. 675; see also no. 198, p. 360.
[111] Only one paper dealer is recorded in the inscriptions, and that
an imperial freedman (VI, 9255: Tiberius Claudius Hermes, *char-
tarius*). Juvenal's Crispinus had been a paper vendor in Egypt
(4, 23-4).

However the papyrus was obtained, the books were copied
and offered for sale in the shops of the *librarii* and *bybliopolae*.
The *librarii* mentioned on the inscriptions are usually from
private establishments and are to be regarded as copyists or
amanuenses; but P. Cornelius Celadus outside the Porta
Trigemina (VI, 9515) was probably an independent dealer,
and there can be no doubt about the *bybliopola*, Sex. Pedu-
caeus Dionysius (9218).[112] As early as the time of Catullus
(58 B. C.) there is a reference to the stores of the book sellers
being closed on the Saturnalia (14, 16-20), and in Cicero's
Second Philippic (21) the story is told how Clodius saved
his life by escaping to the steps of their shops. Although it
has been suggested that at this period the stalls were occupied
not by dealers but by copyists who produced on order,[113] the
lines from Catullus clearly show that certain current works
were kept on hand. The stock of such book dealers, moreover,
could be constantly supplemented by purchases made when the
libraries of wealthy Romans were confiscated and sold at
auction. Atticus himself not only had a large copying establishment but was the publisher, in the modern sense of the
term, of the works of Cicero and of others.[114] Since he had
access to good texts and could secure numerous copies with
ease when his reader, Salvius, dictated to the members of his
trained library staff, it is likely that the scale of production
was rather large.[115] Although there is never any mention of
his shops, there can be no doubt that slaves or freedmen
institores retailed copies of Cicero's speeches from booths
near the Forum.

More definite information about the growing trade in books

[112] Two book sellers are apparently named in VI, 9517 and 9521
(*librarii*). Cf. Suetonius, *Frag.*, p. 134, 18: librarios ante bibliopolas
dictos.
[113] Sommer, " T. Pomponius Atticus und die Verbreitung von
Ciceros Werken," *Hermes*, LXI (1926), 389.
[114] Byrne, *Titus Pomponius Atticus, Chapters of a Biography* (diss.
Bryn Mawr, 1920), 16-18. Other authors, such as Brutus and
Hirtius, whose works he published, are listed there.
[115] See discussion of Clift, *Studies in Pseudepigrapha of the Republic* (unpublished diss. Johns Hopkins, 1937), 13-15. Atticus' large
sheep ranch in Epirus probably supplied the parchment needed for
special de luxe editions.

appears in Horace, from whom we learn that the brothers Sosii, the most celebrated dealers of the time, had one shop near the statue of Vertumnus on the Vicus Tuscus where it joined the Forum and perhaps another by the statue of Janus Medius, the well-known haunt of bankers and speculators.[116] It is Martial, however, who gives us details about the location and appearance of such shops. The dealer Atrectus sold choice volumes trimmed with purple at five denarii ($1.00) in the Argiletum opposite the Forum Transitorium (1, 117, 13-18). The concrete pilasters on either side of his shop were decorated with placards containing samples of the poet's epigrams (*ibid.*, 11-12), an advertising device already used by the enterprising Sosii. The freedman Secundus, moreover, had a shop on the Vicus Sandaliarius, which branched off from the Argiletum near this same Forum (1, 2, 7-8). It is not known where his two other dealers, both Q. Pollius Valerianus (1, 113, 5) and Tryphon (4, 72, 2), had their booths, but they too probably stood in the usual place: the *Argiletanae tabernae*.[117] Martial intimates that Tryphon made considerable profit on his twenty-cent editions of the *Xenia* (13, 3, 1-4).

In the first half of the second century Gellius described the intellectual life of the crowded book stores in the Sigillaria and the Vicus Sandaliarius.[118] Since by this time most of the stores selling books in Rome were concentrated in the street of the Sandal Makers, the suggestion has been made that, with the absorption of part of the Argiletum in the imperial building program, the book dealers had overflowed into the nearby street.[119] All the evidence points to a rather

---

[116] *Ep.*, 1, 20, 1-2: Vertumnum Janumque, liber, spectare videris,
Scilicet ut prostes Sosiorum pumice mundus.
Janus may also refer to the arches in the Forum or to the temple in the Argiletum (see also *Ep.*, 2, 3, 345 and *Serm.*, 1, 4, 71 with Porphyrio's note).

[117] Dziatzko, "Buchhandel," *P.-W.*, III, 979-81.

[118] In the former district the *Annals* of Fabius were on sale (*Noct. Att.*, 5, 4, 1) and also a copy of the second book of the *Aeneid* which was believed to have been Vergil's own (2, 3, 5).

[119] Brewster, *Roman Craftsmen and Tradesmen of the Early Empire*, 1917, 62-4. Peck ("The Argiletum and the Roman Book-Trade," *Classical Philology*, IX [1914], 77-8) argues against this usual assumption.

great concentration of rows of small shops, for the absence of copyright laws, which made it possible for anyone to borrow a roll from a friend's library and to reproduce as many copies as desired, discouraged the emergence of large publishing houses. There are records of no other outstanding men after Atticus who were motivated by friendship and genuine literary interests to devote their wealth to the accurate production and sale of books. Most of the *bybliopolae* of the city were apparently Greek freedmen with small capital.[120]

VII. THE MACHINERY OF DISTRIBUTION

Institores. The craftsmen who sold directly from their combined artisan-sales shops and the freedmen of Greek or Oriental origin who distributed provincial imports from small sales booths supplied most of the needs of this simple economic system. This is the only conclusion that can be reached from the inscriptions.[121] Yet, from the legal sources, it is clear that slave agents (*institores*), who in the inscriptions appear as mere names or perhaps as private artisans in the columbaria of the great households,[122] were constantly entrusted with business enterprises of vast responsibility. The importance of these *institores* is shown by legal protection offered those who negotiated with such slaves.[123] At times, these dependents would be put in charge of sales booths along

---

[120] Dziatzko, *P.-W.*, 982.

[121] Often, as we have seen, several freedmen of one master managed single booths, either working on a commission basis or solely in their own interest. Juvenal (1, 105-6) mentions a freedman who had made a fortune from his chain of five shops.

[122] For example, a slave *aurifex* or *vestiarius* whose inscription is found in the columbarium of a wealthy citizen may not supply the needs of the immediate household, as is usually stated, but may have an independent booth at which he works for the account of his master (see Gummerus, " Industrie und Handel," *P.-W.*, IX, 1457-9; Klingmüller, " Institor," *P.-W.*, IX, 1564).

[123] A slave could be lent capital by his master, the commercial profits belonging to the slave and the annual interest to the master. If the enterprise failed the debts owed the master ranked only with those of other creditors (see *tributoria actio*: *Dig.*, 14, 4). In the cases where the profits fell to the master and the agent received either wages or gifts *institoria actio* could be instigated against the master for the obligations contracted by the slave (*Dig.*, 14, 3).

the front of the house;[124] at others, they would act as hawkers, carrying the wares through the streets or to the home of
customers;[125] often they served as factors for large merchants
who were their masters.[126] Since such slaves are rarely
recorded in the inscriptions and the jurists discuss merely
the degree of their independence, it will never be possible to
define the extent of their activities; but they are the true
middlemen of the city.

Many of these slaves or freedmen were not established in a
taberna: some stood behind a makeshift stand of boards on
the sidewalk; others, by a tripod on a busy corner or near a
column in the Forum.[127] The lengths to which this abuse
could be carried is detailed in Martial's epigram (7, 61)
beginning:

> Abstulerat totam temerarius institor urbem
> Inque suo nullum limine limen erat.

Barbers, innkeepers, cooks, and clothing dealers at Rome
had carried their business so far onto the sidewalk that the
praetor had been forced to proceed on his way through the
gutters. Such "open-air" selling was encouraged by the
erection of porticoes along most of the city streets and of
covered colonnades in public places. The climate might be
added as an additional factor. The famous picture of the
Forum at Pompeii represents this condition with remarkable
clarity: dealers in copper vessels, shoemakers, fruit vendors,

---

[124] See Ulpian (*Dig.*, 14, 3, 3) : *nec multum facit, tabernae sit
praepositus*, etc.
[125] Labeo (*Dig.*, 14, 3, 5, 9) : *si quis pistor servum suum solitus
fuit in certum locum mittere ad panem vendendum*, etc. See also
Dig., 14, 3, 5, 7.
[126] In this capacity sons as well as slaves were employed. See
under *exercitoria actio* and under *institoria actio*. Discussion of this
material is to be found in Warzburg, *Der gewaltfreie Institor im
klassischen römischen Recht* (diss. Freiburg, 1926), 126; Barrow,
Slavery in the Roman Empire, 1928, 105; Humbert, "Institoria
Actio," *D.-S.*, 545.
[127] Magaldi, *Il commercio ambulante a Pompeii*, 1930; Rostovtzeff,
Storia econ., facing 115. See also the shop signs (*N. S.*, 1912, 179),
where racks filled with clothing and shoes crowd the street outside
the booths.

pastry cooks, and wine-testers are all selling their wares before an equestrian statue in the open colonnade.[128]

Pedlers. A further step in the emancipation of the merchant from the confines of the shop was effected by the pedler (*circitor, mercator, ambulator, institor, circumforaneus*). These hawkers played an important rôle in a city where salesmen taking order for future delivery were almost completely unknown.[129] Pedlers of sulphur matches (Mart., 1, 41, 2-5), butchers' boys (*id.,* 6, 64, 21), ice water vendors (Seneca, *Quaest. Nat.,* 4, 13, 8), herb sellers (Pers., 4, 21), pastry salesmen (Mart., 14, 223), and retailers of sausage, warm puddings, and pies (Mart., 1, 41, 6-8, and 9-10) crowded the streets and carried their wares through the arcades of public buildings. Like modern pedlers these salesmen often set no fixed price on their wares but took what they could get from individual purchasers (Sen., *loc. cit.*). Seneca, who lived over a bathing establishment, has given a lively picture of the din produced by the distinctive cries of the sausageman, the cake seller, and the confectioner (*Ep.,* 56, 2)—cries which have persisted in the *voci* and *stese* of the modern Neapolitan macaroni or ravioli vendor.[130] Salesmen sent out by *vestiarii* and *lintearii* went from house to house (*Dig.,* 14, 3, 5, 4); retailers of expensive articles of silver plate carried their wares to the wealthy for display purposes (*Dig.,* 19, 5, 20, 2); and even as early as Ovid's time the pedler at the door had become a private menace.[131]

[128] Reproduced in Mau, 52. It was probably from a clothing dealer such as one of these that the cloak was stolen by Ascyltos and Encolpius (Petr., *Sat.,* 12).

[129] The organization of the potters at La Graufesenque, who produced on orders, is so unusual as to demand special attention (see Gummerus, " Die südgallische Terrasigillata-industrie nach den Graffiti aus la Graufesenque," *Societas Scientiarum Fennica,* III, 3, 1930, 1-21; Grenier, 543-7). In Britain hawkers of pottery, brooches, trinkets, and charcoal went the length and breadth of the island in their homemade carts (Collingwood, 115). Travelling merchants in Italy—both salesmen and buyers—are recorded in the inscriptions: wool dealers from Mutina (*C. I. L.,* XI, 862), a pearl merchant from Rome at Aquileia (Dessau, 7603), etc.

[130] Magaldi, 12-15. Some of these calls are preserved on Roman inscriptions: " mala mulieres, mulieres mea " (" Mercator " in *D.-S.,* fig. 4921).

[131] *Ars Amator.,* 1, 421-2. See also Sen., *de Ben.,* 6, 38, 3; Hor., *Carm.,* 3, 6, 30.

Shop Signs. A clothing dealer on the Vicus Tuscus not only attracted patrons to his shop by hawkers bearing his wares through the streets and by an enticing display along the sidewalk but often by the more restrained advertising device of the shop's sign.[132] Many a wine or specialty store in the city was known simply as *Ad Pinum* (*C. I. L.,* VI, 10035) or *Ad Sorores* IIII (10036). The two pictures from Pompeii showing Mercury protecting the felt factory and Venus fostering the shoe shop are samples of the more elaborate signs,[133] but various smaller reliefs were in common usage. At Rome the large marble relief depicting the female butcher in her bird and fowl store and bearing the famous lines from the first book of Vergil (in a later hand) is probably the most renowned.[134] *Proscriptiones,* often cleverly composed, also drew the attention of the passerby,[135] and even the choice epigrams of a favorite poet were tacked up on the door posts of the shop to lure the literary-minded within (Mart., 1, 117).

Delivery. These conditions in no way alleviated the traffic problems caused by the narrowness of the Roman streets (about 5 to 6.5 m.).[136] As early as the *Lex Julia* attempts to solve these problems had been made by prohibiting wagons within the city after sunrise.[137] Difficulty in delivery occasioned by the absence of such wagons was another feature that fostered the appearance of small shops at every corner: if there had been large bakeries or clothing stores in the city,

---

[132] Riepl, *Das Nachrichtenwesen des Altertums,* 1913, 367, nn. 5-7. Mau, " Aushängeschilder," *P.-W.,* II, 2558-9.

[133] *N. S.,* 1912, 176-181, figs. 2 and 3. An advertisement painted on the side of a shop in which gutter and roof tiles were sold has recently been found (*N. S.,* 1936, 333, and Frank, " Breviora," *A. J. P.,* LVIX [1938], 204-5).

[134] Jahn, pl. 13, 2.

[135] The advertisement of a marble worker at Rome (VI, 9556) reads: *D. M. titulos scribendos vel si quid operis marmorari opus fuerit hic habes.*

[136] Friedländer, *Sittengeschichte Roms,* I, 1922, 6. The Vicus Tuscus was approximately 4.48 m. wide. See also Lehmann-Hartleben, " Städtebau," *P.-W.,* VI, Zweite Reihe, 2069-70.

[137] Sec. 56-61: " no person shall be allowed in the daytime, after sunrise or before the 10th hour of the day, to lead or drive any heavy wagon; except where it shall be requisite for the sake of building the sacred temples of the immortal gods or carrying out the dead " (Hardy's translation in *Roman Laws and Charters,* 1912).

it would have been difficult for the housewife to get to them quickly, and delivery to the individual tenements by the producer was, of course, impossible.

Auctions. No study of methods of distribution employed in the city can fail to take account of the auctioneer, for in the almost complete absence of middleman devices, his work like that of the pedler assumed immense importance.[138]   In Cicero's day the *atria auctionaria* were the scene of constant sales of property confiscated by the state or put under the hammer because of debt (*Leg. Agr.*, 1, 7), and familiar figures in the Atria Licinia, Rome's Auctioneer's Row, were the dissolute young men who had to sell off their personal effects to meet their creditors' demands (*pro Quinct.*, 25). The Licinia are the only rooms known by name, but it is not improbable that there were many others; the seven atria built by Domitan apparently served such a purpose.[139]

Since most of the sources mention the auctioneer's hammer only in connection with state confiscations, we are poorly informed about sales of a more commercial character at Rome. There are still preserved, however, over one hundred fifty wax tablets of L. Caecilius Jucundus, the wealthy auctioneer of Pompeii; [140] and though most of them are receipts for the sales of property (some of them valued at well over $1,000: *C. I. L.,* IV, 3340, 38 and 45), others record sales of slaves (49), of a mule (1), of boxwood (5, *auctio buxiaria*) and of a consignment of Egyptian linen. This *auctio lintiaria Ptolemei Masylli fili Alexsandrini* (100) suggests the possibility that in Rome, as in colonial America, foreign goods might have been

---

[138] Leist, "Auctio," *P.-W.,* II, 2270-72.

[139] For these atria see Chronograph of the year 354 (n. 87 of this chapter). Juvenal (7, 6-7) implies that working in the atria is the same as becoming an auctioneer. This implication is strengthened by the inscription from Superaequum (*C. I. L.,* IX, 3307) in which a rich man builds an *atrium auctionarium* for his town. Many of the atria known from the city, then, may have served this function. In addition to the Atria Licinia the following may be noted: Atrium Traiani (VI, 33808), Atrium Caci (*Reg. Cat.,* Reg. VIII), Atrium Cyclopis, Atrium Maenium, and Atrium Titianum. In the Atrium Sutorium there were probably workrooms and a special sales centre.

[140] Published in *C. I. L.,* IV, Suppl. 1-2; see also Mau, 516-521.

shipped directly to the auctioneer who served as the distributing agent.   Having deducted his customary 1 per cent fee and the sales tax of 1 per cent (5 per cent for slaves) imposed by the state,[141] he sent the proceeds to the merchant abroad—in this case Ptolemeus Masyllus.   Such auctions of imported wares would attract not only the individual consumer but the small shopkeeper who needed to replenish his stock.   Stocks could also be filled when the books, plate, pictures and clothing of estates under judicial process were sold at auction.[142]

Valuable testimony to the importance of the auctioneer's work is given by Martial's humorous equation (6, 8) of the income of one *praeco* to that of two praetors, or four military tribunes, or seven lawyers, or ten poets.   The numerous business ventures of Jucundus and the luxury of his home also indicate the success he found in this calling, and Juvenal is bitter about the lucrative nature of the activities in the *atria auctionaria*.[143]   It is not unlikely that the auctioneers from special sections mentioned in the inscriptions (VI, 1953: *de Subura*; 1950: *de regione Portae Capenae*; *N. S.*, 1911,

[141] The auctioneer's fee is clearly shown on the receipts of Jucundus.   For the sales tax see Tac., *Ann.*, 1, 78 and 2, 42.   Suetonius (*Gaius*, 16) intimates the remission (in 38 A. D.: Dio, 59, 9, 7) applied to only one kind of tax (*ducentesima auctionum*).

[142] Possibly a *circulator* went around to a select clientele announcing the next day's sale and displaying sample articles.   Circulars were also posted, the most famous of which is the unfortunate notice of the bankrupt in Petronius (*Sat.*, 38): "Julius Proculus will sell at auction some of his superfluous stock."   At the opening of the auction the *praeco* had an opportunity to show the power of his notorious lungs in the preliminary announcement of the conditions of sale (Quintilian, *Inst. Orat.*, 1, 12, 17).   The elder Seneca (*Contr.*, 1, praef. 19), in illustration of the prodigious memory of Hortensius, tells how the famous orator sat in the auction rooms through one whole day and at the end was able to repeat in their correct order all the articles sold, the prices, and the buyers ("while the auctioneer's assistants checked him so there would be no mistake").   After the sale a period of several weeks for payments was probably granted, for *coactores argentarii* (collectors of the sums promised at sales) occur frequently in the inscriptions (*C. I. L.*, VI, 9189-90, 33838, etc.).   In fact, Horace's father (*Serm.*, 1, 6, 86-7 and Acro, *ad loc.*) and the grandfather of the Emperor Vespasian (Suet., *Vesp.*, 1) built up their modest fortunes in this way.   See also von Premerstein, "Coactor," *P.-W.*, IV, 126-7.

[143] Juv., 7, 5-7; 3, 33; cf. Quint., *Inst. Orat.*, 11, 2, 24.

398: *a foro*)were prosperous enough to rent rooms in which to hold their sales. There are, however, records of lesser auctioneers who set up their spears on any street corner, summoned buyers with their mighty voice, and disposed of old garments, bookcases, wine jugs, and varied other worthless trinkets.[144]

With the exception of auctioneers, pedlers, or small shopkeepers the sources and inscriptions have little to say about the distributing agents, while wholesale dealers in foods, metal ware, and clothing are scarcely mentioned. Yet the ambiguity of the term *negotiator* and the absence of records of slave or freed *institores* may be concealing some of the middleman machinery. Rather large chains of stores such as those for ready-made clothing, operated by the freedmen of a wealthy master, did, moreover, impose on the patron or his representative some of the functions of a jobber. On the other hand, the persistence of the small-shop system, increased by the traffic problem and the type of architecture at Rome, is nowhere revealed more clearly than in the great Mercato and in the horrea owned by the government. Some regulation of prices and sales conditions undoubtedly existed, but in the disposal of fiscal products coming to the centre of government, the state, in so far as can be judged from the available evidence, seemed content to depend on the services of small independent retailers.

---

[144] Hor., *Ep.*, 2, 3, 419; 1, 7, 63-6; Juv., 7, 9-11.

CONCLUSION

Any study of Roman economics is necessarily qualitative; there are no reliable statistics, no specialists among the sources, no documents of a strictly commercial nature. Because of this meagre material as well as the fundamental simplicity of the economic structure the picture presented is often vague. Yet exact details can be assembled. It may be illuminating to know that clothing for the man in the streets at Rome came from woolen mills in the Po valley, that three hundred grain barges were in passage between Rome and Ostia in one day, that there were over one hundred fifty stalls available for merchants in Nero's portico, or that the Syrian factory at the capital contributed about twenty thousand dollars a year to the branch at Puteoli. Much purely descriptive material of this nature has been presented in the three sections.

Discussions of commerce, trade, and industry in other cities are, in general, applicable to the capital; its position as fiscal centre of the empire apparently resulted in little state control or participation in commerce and trade during the early empire. Food supplies, clothing, and articles of luxury were imported by free merchants, who established their agencies and disposed of their cargoes in the markets by the Tiber in much the same way as at Puteoli. To secure an adequate food supply and a complacent electorate, however, the government induced individual traders, through grants of citizenship rights or exemptions from legal restrictions, to contract with it for carrying the tribute or state-purchased grain, and even aided these independent shipowners by money compensations when in times of scarcity it was forced to maintain a low price for wheat. Not until the period of military anarchy of the third century does compulsion of control in the strict sense appear.

Information about the great mercantile structures erected by the government is far from complete, but none of the available evidence indicates that the state entered trade to

154

dispose of imports coming to the fiscus. Nero's portico, the Basilica Argentaria, Trajan's Mercato, and the numerous horrea all seem to have been occupied by independent merchants, whose activities were restricted only by some official regulation of the sales price of foods and perhaps of other products. The grain tribute necessarily involved the government as one agent in the process of distribution, but it is questionable whether any other saleable tribute in kind was directed to the capital. Because of the unique position of Egypt, however, it is likely that a portion of the products from Alexandrian factories—especially those for papyrus, linen, glass, and perfumes—came in this form even in the early empire. For the third century the practice is well established. As a result of this situation the most positive evidence for state trading has come from the study of Vespasian's erection of the Horrea Piperataria. Even here, however, the extent cannot be defined; there are certainly no indications that private dealers in spices and ointments suffered from state competition.

The assumption that the industrial organization of Rome was unlike that of Pompeii and like that of Alexandria has found no support in the material examined. It must be admitted that tombstones and trade stamps, with which the study was chiefly concerned, undoubtedly centre the attention on small artisan groups. This type of production, however, is confirmed by other evidence: the large numbers of craftsmen in the city, the vigorous trade guilds, and the concentration of workmen in special quarters argue against any theory of factories run by slaves. A consideration of the Marble Plan and of the few remains of tenement houses at Rome has also failed to show essential changes in industrial and commercial quarters. Although the need of expensive equipment and of specially trained artisans fostered manufactories of some size for baking, fulling, and the production of silver plate and luxury furniture, only in the case of brickmaking did large numbers of workmen appear. Yet even here the unit of five or six men was basal. The conditions that resulted in lack of manufacturing on a large scale in the city included not only the absence of metals or fuels nearby, of labor-saving machinery, and of patents to protect trade secrets, but also the Roman law on partnerships, which hindered the concentration of capital and industry, and especially the lack of respect that prevailed in ancient society for the success won from commerce and trade.

INDEX

158   INDEX

institores, 143, 147-9, 153.
insulae, 60-3.
iron, 46-7, 58, 94-5.
ivory, 50, 98.

jewelers, 86-90, 133-5.
Jucundus (L. Caecilius), 73, 151.

labor: in brickmaking, 104-5; in
  building, 84-5; in lamp production, 107-8; in making of lead
  pipes, 109-10.
lamps, 106-9.
lawsuit of fullers, 72.
lead, 45-6.
lead pipes, 109-11.
linen, 34-5.
luxury fabrics, 35, 131.

marble, 39-42.
Marble Plan, 6, 61-2, 113.
margaritarii, 51, 133-5.
markets, 116-7.
Marmorata, 40.
meats, 28-30, 126-8.
Mercato of Trajan, 61, 118-20.
metal work, 86-95, 135-6.
middlemen, 29, 35, 58, 59, 151,
  153.
minium, 99-100.
monopoly, 100, 103, 110, 139, 144.
Monte Testaccio, 20-3, 26, 59.

names of streets, 64-5.
negotiatores, 16, 31, 35-7, 41, 49,
  76, 97, 136, 153.
Nero's portico, 133-4.

oil: annual import, 24; retailers,
  126; varieties, 25-6.
olives, 26.
Ostia, 12, 66.
oysters, 32.

Padua, 33, 64.
Palaemon (Q. Remmius), 18, 129.
papyrus, 55, 100-1, 143-4.
partnerships, 19, 22-3, 59.
pearls, 52, 134-5.
pedlers, 149.
Periplus of the Erythraean Sea,
  51, 52.
Piazzale delle Corporazioni, 14.

Piscina Publica, 127.
pistores, 66, 68.
population, 11.
pork, 28-9.
Praetorian Camp, 125.
purpurarii, 75-7.
Puteoli, 15, 46, 56-7, 140.

river traffic, 12, 14.
Roman law, 59, 112.

Sacra Via, 133-4.
sagarii, 36, 131, 132-3.
sailing vessels, 11, 39.
scale of production, 63, 99, 101,
  155.
Septician ware, 89.
Sequani, 28, 33.
shippers, 22, 58.
shoemaking, 77-9.
shops, 113, 133, 143, 153.
shop signs, 150.
silver, 45.
silversmiths, 90-2.
slave labor, 63-4, 79-80, 112.
spices and ointments, 53-4, 139-
  43.
state trading, 122, 138.
stationes, 55-8.
stevedores, 14, 51.
stone, 37-8.

Trajan's edict (for bakers), 66.
tribute in kind, 21, 24, 52, 54-5,
  120, 139, 140, 144.
truck farms, 26.

unguentarii, 142-3.

vascularii, 90-2.
vegetables, 26-7.
Velabrum, 28, 120.
Vespasian, 138-41, 155.
vestiarii, 73, 128-31.
Vicus Tuscus, 131, 142, 146.
vinarii, 16, 18, 21, 126.

weavers, 70-1.
wine: annual import, 16; distribution, 123; varieties, 17-19,
  20-3.
women, 23, 76, 105.
wood, 42-3, 50.
woolen cloth, 33-4.

ANCIENT ECONOMIC HISTORY

An Arno Press Collection

Andreades, A[ndreas] M[ichael]. **A History of Greek Public Finance.** Vol. I. 1933

Babelon, Ernest [Charles Francois]. **Introduction Générale à l'Étude des Monnaies de l'Antiquité.** 1901

Beloch, Julius. **Die Bevölkerung der Griechisch-Römischen Welt.** 1886

Blümner, Hugo. **Technologie und Terminologie der Gewerbe und Künste bei Griechen und Römern.** Four vols. 1875

Büchsenschütz, B./Blümer, Hugo. **Die Hauptstätten des Gewerbfleisses im Klassischen Alterthume/Die Gewerbliche Thätigkeit der Völker des Klassischen Alterthums.** Two vols. in one. 1869

Davies, Oliver. **Roman Mines in Europe.** 1935

Finley, Moses I., editor. **The Bücher-Meyer Controversy.** 1979

[Finley, Moses I., editor.] **Second International Conference of Economic History.** Volume I: Trade and Politics in the Ancient World. 1965

Francotte, Henri. **Les Finances des Cités Grecques.** 1909

Francotte, Henri. **L'Industrie dans la Grèce Ancienne.** Two vols. 1900/1901

Friedländer, Ludwig. **Roman Life and Manners under the Early Empire.** Four vols. [1908-1913]

Fustel de Coulanges, [Numa Denis]. **Le Colonat Romain.** 1885

Gernet, L[ouis]. **L'Approvisionnement d'Athènes en Blé au Ve et au IVe Siècle.** 1909

Graindor, Paul. **Un Milliardaire Antique.** 1930

Gren, Erik. **Kleinasien und der Ostbalkan in der Wirtschaftlichen Entwicklung der Römischen Kaiserzeit.** 1941

Halkin, Léon. **Les Esclaves Publics chez les Romains/Le Père d'Horace a-t-il été Esclave Public?** 1897/1935

Heichelheim, Fr[itz M.]. **Wirtschaftliche Schwankungen der Zeit von Alexander bis Augustus.** 1930

Herfst, Pieter. **Le Travail de la Femme dans la Grèce Ancienne.** 1922

Jacob, Oscar. **Les Esclaves Publics à Athènes.** 1928

Klíma, Otakar. **Mazdak.** 1957

Korver, Jan. **De Terminologie van het Crediet-Wezen in het Grieksch.** 1934

Krauss, Samuel. **Talmudische Archäologie.** Three vols. 1910/1911/1912

Kuenzi, Adolphe. ΕΠΙΔΟΣΙΣ. 1923

Loane, Helen Jefferson. **Industry and Commerce of the City of Rome.** 1938

Mickwitz, Gunnar. **Geld und Wirtschaft im Römischen Reich.** 1932

Mickwitz, Gunnar. **Die Kartellfunktionen der Zünfte.** 1936

Moritz, L.A. **Grain-Mills and Flour in Classical Antiquity.** 1958

Mossé, Claude. **La Fin de la Démocratie Athénienne/La Vie Économique d'Athènes au IVe Siècle.** 1962/1972

Nissen, Heinrich. **Italische Landeskunde.** Two vols. in three. 1883/1902

Persson, Axel W. **Staat und Manufaktur in Römischen Reiche.** 1923

Préaux, Claire. **L'Économie Royale des Lagides.** 1939

Reil, Theodor. **Beiträge zur Kenntnis des Gewerbes im Hellenistischen Ägypten.** 1913

Reizler, Kurt. **Über Finanzen und Monopole im Alten Griechenland.** 1907

Robertis, Francesco M. de/Nörr, Dieter. **Lavoro e Lavoratori nel Mondo Romano/ Zur Sozialen und Rechtlichen Bewertung der Freien Arbeit in Rom.** 1963/1965

Rostovtzeff, Michael. **A Large Estate in Egypt in the Third Century B.C.** 1922

Salvioli, G. **Le Capitalisme dans le Monde Antique.** 1906

Schmidt, Alfred. **Drogen und Drogenhandel im Altertum.** 1924

Schneider, A[nna]. **Die Anfänge der Kulturwirtschaft.** 1920

Thompson, E.A. **A Roman Reformer and Inventor.** 1952

Urbach, E.E. **The Laws Regarding Slavery.** 1964

van Groningen, B[ernhard] A[braham], editor. **Aristote: Le Second Livre de l'Economique.** 1933

Vandier, Jacques. **La Famine dans l'Égypte Ancienne.** 1936

Waltzing, J[ean] —P[ierre]. **Étude Historique sur les Corporations Professionnelles chez les Romains.** Four vols. 1895/1896/1899/1900

Weber, Max. **Die Römische Agrargeschichte.** 1891

Wilcken, Ulrich. **Griechische Ostraka.** Two vols. 1899